Erica

NOVANT HEALTH

Dear team members,

One of the things I am most proud of when I talk about Novant Health is our people credo. Leading an organization that is inclusive, purpose-driven and united in our commitment makes my job a privilege. It refuels me to hear remarkable stories, day in and day out, highlighting your dedication to our mission, vision, values and your compassion for the people we care for. This is why I get up each day and come here, excited about our work.

Finding those things that fill us up and keep us going is vital to fulfilling our core values. As human beings, we can't find compassion for others if we are tired and overwhelmed. We may not be as supportive or accepting of differences when we're running on empty, just trying to get through the week. In contrast, when we are replenished in body, mind and spirit, we fulfill our promise to our patients, our loved ones and ourselves.

I am excited to share with you our 2018 Novant Health Reads selection, *Type R: Transformative Resilience for Thriving in a Turbulent World*. I hope that this book will help you develop your resiliency skills and provide you with the tools you need to be your best self here and at home.

Novant Health is a community of remarkable people. I see your passion and your commitment every day. By building resiliency skills, we become that much better. Thank you for participating in this year's program. I look forward to hearing your thoughts, ideas and stories as you share how *Type R* impacts you.

Carl S. Armato

Carl S. Armato
President and CEO, Novant Health

TYPE R

Transformative Resilience *for* Thriving *in a* Turbulent World

AMA MARSTON *and*
STEPHANIE MARSTON

PUBLICAFFAIRS
New York

The names and identifying characteristics of some of the interviewees in this book have been changed to protect their privacy.

PublicAffairs
Hachette Book Group
1290 Avenue of the Americas, New York, NY 10104
www.publicaffairsbooks.com
@Public_Affairs

Printed in the United States of America

First Edition: January 2018

Published by PublicAffairs, an imprint of Perseus Books, LLC, a subsidiary of Hachette Book Group, Inc. The PublicAffairs name and logo is a trademark of the Hachette Book Group.

The publisher is not responsible for websites (or their content) that are not owned by the publisher.

Print book interior design by Amy Quinn.

Library of Congress Cataloging-in-Publication Data

Names: Marston, Ama, author. | Marston, Stephanie, author.
Title: Type R : transformative resilience for thriving in a turbulent world / Ama Marston, Stephanie Marston.
Description: First Edition. | New York : PublicAffairs, 2018. | Includes bibliographical references.
Identifiers: LCCN 2017025476| ISBN 9781610398060 (hardback) | ISBN 9781610398077 (ebook)
Subjects: LCSH: Resilience (Personality trait) | Stress management. | Decision making. | BISAC: PSYCHOLOGY / Mental Health. | SELF-HELP / Stress Management. | BUSINESS & ECONOMICS / Decision-Making & Problem Solving.
Classification: LCC BF698.35.R47 M37 2018 | DDC 155.9/042--dc23
LC record available at https://lccn.loc.gov/2017025476

ISBNs: 978-1-61039-806-0 (hardcover), 978-1-61039-807-7 (ebook)

LSC-C

10 9 8 7 6 5 4 3 2 1

We dedicate this book to family,
both ours and yours,
and to the future of a larger, global family.

Contents

PROLOGUE
1

CHAPTER 1
Meeting the Rising Tides in a Turbulent and Changing World
11

CHAPTER 2
Transformative Resilience and the Adversity Sweet Spot
29

CHAPTER 3
Type R: The Mindset for Our Time
51

CHAPTER 4
Harnessing the Storm: The Type R Characteristics
67

CHAPTER 5
Transformers: The Type R Individual
97

CHAPTER 6
Navigating Uncharted Waters: The Type R Leader
121

CHAPTER 7
We're All in It Together: The Type R Organization
151

CHAPTER 8
A Bridge Over Troubled Water: The Type R Family
177

CHAPTER 9
Type R in Action
199

ACKNOWLEDGMENTS
217

NOTES
221

INDEX
233

Prologue

OUR WORLD HAS become an increasingly volatile place over the last several years. With our morning coffee and the first dose of the day's news, we're confronted by unprecedented world events, from terrorism, gun violence, and cyber-attacks to global pandemics. With businesses facing global competition and economies vulnerable to repeated crises, our careers are unstable. Today many of us face layoffs, the stress of being expected to do more work with fewer people, and decreased pay and benefits. Then there's the stress of daily life itself—births, deaths, illnesses, breakups. Balancing work and family, shouldering the strain of economic concerns, and finding ways to distinguish ourselves in a world of growing competition. It's a list to keep any of us up at night.

The challenge for most of us isn't to outpace stress, adversity, and momentous change; it's to meet them head-on. It's to learn how to deal with uncertainty not as a passing state but as a condition of life. That said, there has never been a greater need for us to grow and create opportunity from adversity.

With the challenges we face, we need a new generation of thinking—one that brings a fresh focus on coping with an ever-changing and turbulent world and transforming ourselves to better thrive in this new reality.

The difference between those who fold and those who flourish is not resilience in the traditional sense of the word, but one better suited for these tumultuous times: Transformative Resilience, the ability to learn, grow, and spring forward. These individuals, leaders, businesses, families, and even communities that turn challenges into opportunity are what we call Type Rs.

By drawing on decades of research across the disciplines of psychology, sociology, behavioral economics, neuroscience, business, and current affairs, we have come to believe that Type Rs are our future and that Transformative Resilience is the new paradigm for our time.

Yet, these new concepts are not simply born out of theory and research. Our own journey has been one of mother and daughter but also one of partners in Transformative Resilience from early on.

Stephanie's Story

In the mid-1970s my husband, Derrick, my daughter, Ama, and I were living on a farm in an isolated area of British Columbia. As winter neared we piled into our maroon Volkswagen van for a trip to Spokane, Washington, 325 miles away, to stock up on staples. Ama, who was three years old, and I decided to climb onto the plywood bed in the back to read *The Very Hungry Caterpillar* and quickly fell asleep.

We were driving down a remote highway when we hit a patch of ice. A tremendous jolt woke me as our van slid off the road and tumbled to the bottom of a ravine. Suddenly, I was suspended between complete chaos and absolute silence—a moment that seemed to go on forever. When the van finally landed on its side amid the dense brush and fallen leaves, I tried to pull myself up, but an excruciating pain shot down my back. My sock-covered feet were contorted unnaturally and I couldn't move my legs.

Derrick crawled to my side. "Where's Ama?" I screamed.

"She was thrown under the dashboard, but she's okay," he reassured me, though he was shaken. "I'm going to take her up to the road and see if I can find help."

When the paramedics finally arrived several hours later, they rushed me to the hospital. X-rays were taken and I was prepared for surgery. What they didn't tell me was that the breaks in my right foot were so severe, and the circulation so impaired, that the doctors were planning to amputate.

With little time to spare, Derrick spoke with my father, a doctor, who told him to refuse to allow such drastic measures. The surgical team operated on my other leg and repaired my shattered ankle with pins. They would monitor my foot to see whether the circulation returned. My back injuries would also be left on their own to heal. But the doctors told me they doubted I would be able to walk again.

For months I lay in a hospital bed in my childhood bedroom in New Jersey with both legs in casts from foot to groin. Derrick started work at a local business, and my mother took care of Ama and me while I healed. The accident had fractured more than my body. The images I'd crafted of myself as a woman who could live off the land and off the grid had been shattered as well.

It was during this time that I began to surrender to something that was emerging in me. I had glimpsed a larger sense of what I wanted my life to be about. It was as if there, in my childhood home, I was given a new beginning.

In the afternoons, home from nursery school, Ama would tiptoe into my room and carefully climb onto the bed and curl up next to me. The most we could do together was watch *Sesame Street* or read a story, but we comforted each other.

After seven months in bed, I was ready to learn to walk again. It took weeks of grueling exercises and it came in fits and starts. Most days were deeply frustrating. But the doctor's first words to me—that I'd live life in a wheelchair—echoed in my head and propelled me forward. I was determined to live a full life and raise my daughter. Finally, one day, I sat at the parallel bars, preparing to go from one end to the other. "I can do this," I thought. I locked the wheels on my chair, lifted myself up, grasped the bars, and gingerly set my feet on the mat. Slowly, proudly, I began to take my first steps. Tears welled up in my eyes. The other patients around me cheered and clapped. I was on my way.

I had fought to regain the physical strength I had always assumed I could count on, and in the process, something within me was fundamentally changed. Perhaps it was being confronted with how vulnerable I was, how fragile and precious my life was. Perhaps it was having to fight for something I had taken for granted. But I knew that I had to start truly living. I discovered a renewed sense of compassion and appreciation, and a desire to make a contribution to the lives of others. And so the accident planted the seed for my future career as a psychotherapist, with a focus on helping people deal with stress.

Ama's Story

Three decades after our car accident, in my mid-thirties, it was me on extended bed rest. I was in London, where I have lived for the past several years and had recently started my own strategy and leadership consultancy.

As I looked out the window into the morning light, I had my usual impulse to throw myself into the day with determination. But as I turned over in bed, a jolt of pain traveled down my back to my toes and reminded me that there was nowhere for me to go. I had slipped multiple discs in my back recently during one of the most stressful periods of my life.

Just three weeks earlier, in the middle of the night in a Bangkok hospital I had stood over my father. Tears streamed down my face as I fought exhaustion from worry and jet lag.

"Where's Ama? Is she okay?" my dad asked, panicky in a morphine-induced daze.

"I'm here, Dad. I'm fine." I hadn't been to Thailand, where he now lived, in over a year, and felt like I was in a strange dream as I realized he had flashed back thirty years to our car crash in Canada.

"Dad. You hurt yourself in an accident. You're going to be okay, but you have to stay where you are," I said, as I held him up, struggling to make sure that he didn't try to step off the edge of the hospital bed. I was afraid to remind him that, in a strange twist of fate, his right foot had been severely injured in a car accident. With few good options, he had chosen amputation.

Taking it all in, I was struck by his mortality and by my own powerlessness in the situation. Perhaps if my life were not in such chaos, I thought, I might have been able to offer more support and even could have stayed longer as he healed.

But I'd been pushing myself for months, if not years. A fundamental change was coming that went beyond my recent decision to leave my job and start a consulting business. I was struggling under the weight of the financial crisis and the extreme stress of qualifying to renew my UK work permit while immigration policies became increasingly stringent. Work was a constant sprint. I was advising global leaders and stretching to expand into the private sector. Meanwhile, many of the early projects that supported me came from the nonprofit work I had been doing before, taking on assignments aimed at solving the world's largest problems on short deadlines and shoestring budgets.

But suddenly it wasn't the world that needed caring for. It was my family and loved ones. And it was the idea of a more fulfilling personal life and future that needed my attention.

"How did my life get to this point?" I cried over the phone to my mom back home in the United States.

"The good news is that you're talented and have lots of options to choose what you want to do next and your dad is strong and will heal," she reassured me.

But I could hear the worry in her voice and was reminded of the strain *she* was under. I was so proud of her as she ventured into new territory as the founder of a stress and mental wellness start-up after years as a psychotherapist and corporate consultant. But I also worried for her as she faced the financial crisis and rode the highs and lows of becoming an entrepreneur.

As the pressure, bad news, and worry coursed through me, the tension found a home in my lower back. I could only hold up so much of the sky before crumbling under the weight.

For six months, I was forced to let go of control, adapt, and rebuild while my back healed. Hope was measured in the amount of sunlight reflecting off the wall across from my bedroom, in the small piles of restorative vitamins I faithfully downed, and in the number of steps I could take around the block, clutching my lower back and listening to Missy Elliott as I tried to maintain a sense of humor and some semblance of my more vibrant self. And it was measured by the daily calls my mom made to check on me.

When I was finally allowed to swim, hope was measured by my ability to focus on my breath and chase away doubt as my body slowly grew stronger. It became an exercise in being who I was and where I was in life.

From our respective beds, my dad and I called each other frequently. To my surprise, the accident had helped him develop a positive outlook and lessons he shared with me. "I realized I had a choice—I could give up or I could fight for this life and see what this experience has to teach me," he said. "You have to listen to your body telling you to slow down and take care of yourself, Ama. Take this time to ask, 'What's most important to me and what do I want next?'"

* * *

John F. Kennedy said, “There are risks and costs to action. But they are far less than the long range risks of comfortable inaction.” For both of us, in times of crisis, change, and stress, inaction was not an option. We knew we had to adapt and evolve.

But we've also come to the conclusion that, though resilience is important, it's not enough. There's no going back to who or where we were before challenging times. “Bouncing back” is not only a poor choice; it's often not possible. For us it was clear that the only choice was to use these challenges to our advantage and continue to grow.

After a handful of particularly challenging years personally and professionally, in 2013 our conversations began to crystallize into the idea for this book. We discussed how dramatically the world had changed from the one the Boomers were born into. Now the challenges we face are often not just personal or professional, but global. We talked about how Ama's generation, Gen X, as well as Millennials have been affected by the ubiquity of digital technology and social media along with the multiple crises—global terrorism, climate change, and the financial crisis—that have shaped the way they experience everyday events and that have sent shock waves through all aspects of their lives.

We see it all around us. The number of Americans affected by stress and adversity is unprecedented, with 49 percent of people surveyed recently by the Robert Wood Johnson Foundation reporting that they'd had a major stressful event or experience in the past year.[1] And research from the American Psychological Association shows that younger people, women, and people of color are facing even larger pressures.[2]

This book is a culmination of our personal and professional interests and significant expertise in how stresses have converged in a unique and challenging way and why so many people don't just cope with but grow from adversity.

Throughout the book, we share stories of Type R individuals, leaders, businesses, teams, families, and even communities that exemplify Transformative Resilience combined with research across a range of disciplines.

And, at the heart of this book is a fundamental question: How can we leverage change and hardship into opportunity as individuals and carry that progress into the world as a contribution to the collective? We hope that you will join us on the journey of finding meaning in your own challenges as we did in ours.

That said, this book isn't intended as a self-help guide for the chronically stressed and habitually challenged—it's not meant as "How to Adversity-Proof Your Life," say, or "Thirty Days to a More Positive You." On the contrary, it's an investigation of this moment in history and why the realities that we're living are different from the past and bring with them unique challenges and pressures. With that in mind, we show how individuals and groups of people of all ages who build a foundation of Transformative Resilience are better able to operate in and positively affect the world.

First, we look at why past approaches to resilience that put our individual lives and global challenges into separate siloes no longer work and how the realities that we now live require a melding of the two. We examine how many of the foundations that we rely on to navigate these chaotic times are rooted in outdated beliefs that leave us poorly equipped for today's challenges. And we look at why the ability to reframe stress and adversity is an essential skill that all of us need to learn and how Transformative Resilience offers tools that previous thinking does not.

Next, we look at the Type R mindset and skills, the characteristics that define them, and how Type Rs embrace uncertainty and accept—even welcome—change, failure, and disruption. We also look at how individuals can evolve through the TR Journey, a six-stage process that propels us to turn adversity, stress, and change into opportunity.

While we begin the book by focusing on individuals, in the second half we explore how individuals can use their growth to contribute to the world in a way that creates a positive impact. We then look at Type R leaders and organizations and how they cultivate and leverage Type R Vision and cultures in order to be more effective and have a greater impact. We also explore how we create Transformative Resilience at home while balancing the demands of the change that is taking place in the world with our individual needs and those of our families.

And, finally, we propose steps for putting this new knowledge into action across the various roles that we play, from tackling global and national challenges to juggling our individual needs, building careers and organizations, taking on leadership roles, and caring for our families.

We hope you'll come to see Transformative Resilience and the Type R tools as fundamental for negotiating our increasingly interconnected, fast-paced, and turbulent world. We offer this book to you as a road map to help you navigate these demanding times, fraught with historic challenges as well as immense opportunities.

CHAPTER 1

Meeting the Rising Tides in a Turbulent and Changing World

And onward full tilt we go, pitched and wrecked and absurdly resolute, driven in spite of everything to make good on a new shore.

Barbara Kingsolver

THE SOUND OF waves breaking on the beach is familiar, calming—and yet it tells of impending danger. For centuries the sea has cradled the tiny Carteret Atoll in the South Pacific near Papua New Guinea, but now it eats away at the tropical paradise where Ursula Rakova was born. Ownership of one island was passed from Rakova's grandmother to her mother and on to her. And though she would like to pass the island on to her own daughter, the atoll is disappearing under the waves—one hut, one village, one island at a time.

Since the 1950s, the sea level has risen at a phenomenal rate. Originally, the Carterets were six islands. Then one of them was split in half by the water, making seven. In recent years, the residents have ringed the shores with rock and clamshell barriers in a futile effort to hold back the rising tides. "The sea that we love to swim in is now turning against us," Rakova said. "Our shorelines are eroding so fast. The island is getting smaller and smaller. We have lost at least 40 percent of our land. . . . Year in, year out, every day, it is a struggle for my people."[1]

They have lost their staple food crop as saltwater has turned vegetable plots into swampy breeding grounds for malaria-carrying mosquitoes. Wells have been contaminated. Fish and other seafood are getting harder to find. All that is left is coconut trees. The islanders now have to rely on the government of Papua New Guinea for food. Four hundred years of inhabitance is about to end.

But the community has not lost hope. The Carterets' Council of Elders has entrusted Rakova with planning the community's future, in part because of her years of studies in social work and public administration and her work with international development organizations. She's now leading a permanent resettlement effort. Some two thousand residents from the atoll will be relocated to the mainland in the Autonomous Region of Bougainville, three hours away by boat.

It's Rakova's hope that the younger people who are relocating will be able to start a vibrant new community and help support the older generation who don't want to leave their birthplace.

The local community in Bougainville hails from the same clan as the islanders and has luckily been welcoming. In 2009 the first group of island families—eighty-six people in total—moved into their new homes and started farming again. "People knew that they must move, but there [was] apprehension. They didn't know what was on the other side. They had an inner [fear] about security. The residents asked, 'If we move, what will happen to us?'"

But as time goes on, people are adjusting to their new lives. One of the first steps has been becoming "good new neighbors" and ensuring that locals also benefit from the latest developments and outside support the relocated families receive. The new residents have cleared and planted gardens and are growing enough to feed their community, sell the surplus, and share with those still living on the atoll. And they are raising funds to complete the second settlement of twenty houses that will accommodate another two hundred people.

One of the things that gives Rakova the most hope is that her people can become self-sufficient and can maintain their identity. She doesn't want them to become dependent on the charity of others and believes that producing organic cocoa provides a viable economic future.

In 2014 Rakova founded a company called Bougainville Cocoa Net Limited to create a means for her people to earn an income. As of early 2016, they had planted over thirty-one thousand cocoa trees on their land, built a processing plant for the cocoa beans, and set their sights on planting a hundred thousand trees. "Nobody has stepped in to save us," she explained. "We just have to go ahead and save ourselves."

For Rakova, autonomy also means supporting her people in maintaining their cultural identity. "We are moving away, but not completely. We want to maintain cultural connectedness," she said. "We want to move with dignity. We are proud of our inheritance and we want to keep that."

Where others may have simply relocated and tried to get back to "normal" life, Rakova is dedicated to making sure that the experience of the Carteret settlers and the challenges that they've faced provide a foundation for new opportunity and growth for her community. But she also wants to amplify that growth and the lessons they've learned to ensure that they benefit others. One way that she and the Elders are working toward that is by offering for the detailed plans they have drawn up as the first environmental refugees to serve as a model for other communities that are "on the move." The Carteret Islanders hope this will allow others to relocate on their own terms, while doing so safely.

Welcome to the Era of Uncertainty

Although most of us aren't facing the imminent disappearance of our homes, as Rakova is, we're all living in a world with mounting challenges we haven't dealt with before while also juggling the stresses and strains of normal life. The changes taking place shake the foundations of our personal and family lives, our organizations, leaders, and society more broadly. They lead many of us in different parts of the world to ask some of the same basic questions: Can I provide for myself and my family? Will we be safe and have a decent quality of life? And what will happen to our environment and the places where we live?

While the crises and challenges of the past were often readily identifiable, much of what tests us today is less localized and visible in large part because of unprecedented and rapid globalization and the increased use of technologies that unify us across borders. But we are also bound together by challenges like climate change and security threats that are both forged by and responses to the increasingly transnational lifestyles we lead now tying us together.

The extent to which progress has been uneven not only between countries but also within them is catching up with us in ways that will either set us back decades or propel us ahead, depending on the choices that we make.

As Nobel laureate economist Joseph Stiglitz pointed out, trust in the governments and international institutions that have been architects of globalization has increasingly come into question because of a lack of transparency, causing political turbulence and division. At this juncture, the question becomes, Do we turn to the past or look to the future and evolve in the face of aging governments, growing and ever more diverse populations, and mounting environmental and economic pressures?

"Citizens now understand that globalization matters. And they want a voice," Stiglitz said.[2] This is no surprise as we approach a critical moment for examining the forces and the rules that govern our lives and either strengthen or undermine our social fabric—from work to education to health to the environmental and financial regulations that guide business and chart a course for economic and social development.

And at the same time we're being stretched in unprecedented ways on multiple fronts. For instance, in the 2000s, American multinational corporations cut their workforce in the United States by 2.9 million employees while hiring 2.4 million workers overseas, including highly skilled foreign laborers.[3] This growing global competition for jobs, combined with technology, means that many people are now constantly reachable and as a result they now work longer hours. We're expected to be accessible at all times of the day across time zones. And, as a result, many of us are feeling more and more stressed.

Add to that the reality of the changing environment. Rakova's island isn't the only place facing rising sea levels. The bulk of the world's twenty largest cities—Los Angeles, New York, Rio de Janeiro, and Mumbai, to name a few—are built on low-lying land exposed to rising tides and battering storms linked to climate change. And climate change more generally is expected to displace millions from their homes. Already, an average of sixty-two thousand people have been displaced every day since 2008 as a result of climate- and weather-related disasters, a significant increase from decades prior.[4] It's not a matter of whether change is coming. It's a matter of when.

But climate isn't the only issue turning up the heat, so to speak. Although many think of economic inequality as a distant issue, it's knocking on our own back door. Today some of the

CEOs of the world's largest corporations earn five hundred times more than their average worker.[5] And three and a half billion people share between them the same amount of wealth as the world's top eighty wealthiest people.[6]

Amid this mounting pressure across communities, cities, and regions, the impacts become personal for individuals who see their daily realities changing, like Rakova. These global challenges come atop the stresses we naturally face at different stages of our lives—from births to deaths, divorces, illnesses, and job changes—and in some cases amplify them.

Case in point is the global financial crisis. It has touched millions of lives, leading to job loss and, in many cases, loss of homes. Although a number of factors contribute, the mounting stress of economic pressure in people's lives is all too obvious.

Both the financial crisis and economic inequality have diminished options and opportunities for young people, who have quickly become the poorest age group in America. They face skyrocketing costs of living, disposable income that is scarcely higher than it was thirty years ago both in the United States and in Europe, and over $1 trillion in student debt in the United States. As a result, 46 percent of Millennials have been forced to move back into their childhood homes.

Carla, age thirty-two, returned to her parents' home in the United States multiple times after college, living there off and on as she tried to find a job that would pay her enough to live independently. She admitted there were upsides to living at home, but keeping her mother apprised of her whereabouts was a challenge. "I was an adult who had already lived on my own, and I needed to be treated as such," Carla explained. She finished graduate school and no longer lives with her parents, although she fears that if she doesn't find a job immediately, she may have to move home again.[7]

People of all ages have also begun to question our ability to shape a world we want to live in or raise a family in and worry about how our actions reflect our personal beliefs. For instance, NASA scientist James Hansen acutely feels both his duty as a scientist and the challenges of making change. "I have been described as the grandfather of climate change," he told the *Guardian* in 2009. "In fact, I am just a grandfather and I do not want my grandchildren to say that Grandpa understood what was happening but didn't make it clear."[8]

In the past few years alone, the record number of violent conflicts has had an unparalleled impact on the world's children.[9] We sat, seemingly helpless, watching on TV as schools were bombed in Gaza and hundreds of schoolgirls were kidnapped by insurgents in Nigeria. Experiences like these place our core beliefs at odds with our actions (or inactions), making us question our sense of self and purpose: Am I not a person who believes every child should be safe and healthy and allowed to have a childhood? And yet I'm here watching the news and not doing anything, we ask.

In a 2016 public talk in London, award-winning journalist and theologian Krista Tippett pointed out that areas of brilliance around our globe are lighting up with possibilities that have never been available to us before, and yet we're equally met with unparalleled recklessness, destructive potential, and new challenges. This means that we have to grapple both individually and collectively to find better ways to live in this new world and ultimately build a foundation for prospering.

As Leo Tolstoy once said, "Everyone thinks of changing the world, but no one thinks of changing himself." Increasing our own abilities and transforming ourselves is a way we can contribute to the world as individuals as we collectively bring those skills into our families, our leadership, our businesses and institutions, and even our nations.

We can't turn a blind eye to the structural, economic, and social change that must happen to address the global challenges we face. And at the same time, we must ask ourselves, How do we increase our abilities for progress and those of our loved ones in a world of growing uncertainty? How do we ensure that our communities, our livelihoods, and our economies prosper? These conversations are taking place at every level—from the personal to the professional to the global—and everywhere—among PTAs and city planners, at dinner tables and in corporate boardrooms, and among friends, colleagues, and business and political leaders.

As we grapple with these questions, we can't go back in our personal or our shared histories when our lives are disrupted, when we find ourselves challenged, or when we are shocked by difficult new realities. Yet many of the ways in which we talk about these issues are linked to old definitions that fall short of delivering the wide-reaching conceptual change essential to propel us forward. With the challenges we face, we need a new generation of thinking—one that focuses on coping with a volatile world and transforming ourselves into people who can thrive in the new reality, both individually and collectively.

Bouncing Back or Springing Forward?

Nothing less than a revolution is taking place in the ways we think about our responses to adversity. Most people think of the ideal as recovering or bouncing back. They think that people will return to who they were before challenging times. But this overlooks the human capacity and necessity to change, improve, and transform.

Given the pace and ubiquity of change, stress, and overwhelm that we are all facing, getting back to the baseline—to the status quo—isn't enough.

While others have argued for the benefit of "bouncing back," we believe that Transformative Resilience (TR), our capacity to experience a demonstrable positive transformation through adversity and change and ultimately make a contribution to our larger community, is the only way forward. This means revising the assumptions that we have lived by for years, starting with the stories we tell about change, adversity, and stress and the way we choose to frame them.

For many of those who most successfully weather challenging times, the key is becoming Type R and adopting the Type R mindset and skills. (We explore the collection of characteristics that enable Transformative Resilience in greater depth in Chapters 3 and 4 and discuss it throughout the book.) Yet, for years, we've treated people who struggle with change or go through stressful life events as if they have a "problem." As a result, we often focus on the negative side of challenges. Indeed, despite the work of a number of experts who highlight growth from adversity, we continue to see challenges as difficult or unpleasant situations or misfortunes to be avoided rather than as opportunities toward which we turn.

Throughout history people have called upon adversity to thrive. Ludwig van Beethoven wrote his Ninth Symphony late in life when he was almost completely deaf. Despite critical illness and his lack of hearing, he called the finale of the symphony "Ode to Joy," reviving a poem by Friedrich Schiller, which the poet had considered a failure. Beethoven conducted the premiere with his eyes closed, and he continued even after the orchestra had completed the performance and the audience had erupted in an uproar of applause. Tears filled his eyes when one of the choir stepped forward and turned him to face the adoring concertgoers, who shouted "Bravo!" and showered him with five standing ovations. Beethoven could hear neither the orchestra nor the audience. But in that moment, not despite his hardship but because of it, his accomplishment and satisfaction were all the greater.

We shy away from adversity, even though some of the greatest ideas, art, and inventions—from Albert Einstein's theory of relativity to Claude Monet's Impressionist masterpiece *Water Lilies* to the microcomputer invented by Steve Wozniak—have come from individuals who evolved as a result of disruption, discomfort, and hardship. Without persistent, inspired, determined, creative people, the world would not have the richness of:

Charles Darwin's theory of evolution
Sir Isaac Newton's theory of gravity
The Beatles' album *Sgt. Pepper's Lonely Hearts Club Band*
Vincent Van Gogh's *Sunflowers*
J. K. Rowling's Harry Potter books
Frida Kahlo's world-famous self-portrait paintings
Dr. Seuss's *Green Eggs and Ham*
Steven Spielberg's *E.T.*, *Jaws*, and *Schindler's List*
Thomas Edison's light bulb

All of these people and many more are a reminder of the creative power of adversity. Transformative Resilience frames challenge as an opportunity rather than as a problem. It leads to new approaches and questions about how to best address an issue. It asks, What other doors might open for me? What other things might I do? What changes do I need to make? It isn't simply what happens to us but how we respond to what happens that has the greatest effect on the trajectory of our lives after adversity.

But TR is about more than just navigating trauma and hardship. It's about embracing change—something that many of us struggle with, given the speed with which contemporary life and the world move—and using it to our advantage.

Part of this requires letting go of the notion that we will find "balance" and instead embracing the world's numerous imbalances. "Increasingly instead of trying to find an equilibrium in a planet that's out of balance, we also have to try and manage with the unbalances, the imbalances," pointed out author Andrew Zolli, who works on social change and resilience. "We have to manage in a world that's intrinsically out of order."[10]

It's an ongoing process of adapting and strategically letting go—discovering what works, what's useful, and what no longer serves us.

Business as Usual Isn't Working

Increasingly, we have to learn to manage in a world that is out of balance and adapt to change and new realities to achieve a greater level of functioning. Yet we continue to operate on the basis of outdated assumptions and beliefs that hold us back and keep us from developing the mindsets and skills required for our new world. Four obstacles stand out as being particularly limiting to our ability to develop Transformative Resilience.

Obstacle to TR #1: Operating the Same Way We Always Have in the Face of Change

In Tulare County, California, in 2014 the Gallegos family, like others in the area, could no longer flush their toilets, fill a glass of drinking water from the tap, wash dishes, or bathe due to a lack of water. The hundreds of dollars they spent at the laundromat and on paper plates had eaten up their budget for their ten-year-old daughter's after-school activities and for their household expenses. Yolanda Serrato, another area resident who was living in equally challenging circumstances, said, "You don't think of water as a privilege until you don't have it anymore." She added, "We were very proud of making a life here for ourselves, for raising children here. We never ever expected to live this way."[11]

California's drought is just one example of what happens when we try to maintain the status quo in the face of change. The devastating drought that took place from 2011 to 2017 was the worst the state has seen in 120 years, if not longer. But for many it was background noise. For years, farm practices remained unchanged.

City-dwellers continued to water lawns, fill swimming pools, and groom golf courses. Finally, Governor Jerry Brown passed mandatory water reductions in 2015. Without widespread action to address the situation and the interlinkages between water use in urban and rural parts of the state, it was difficult for families in some areas to survive, let alone prosper.

But it's not just local residents who have been affected. Between one-third and one-half of the fruit and vegetables sold in the United States are grown in California, and the state exports large amounts to other parts of the world.[12] Reduced food availability and rising food prices affect the quantity and quality of what shows up on millions of dinner tables across the nation. In 2017, the governor declared the emergency over, but he warned that the next drought could be just around the corner and that ongoing water conservation and resource management must be the way of life for the foreseeable future.

Denying change, rather than adopting the TR approach of embracing it, only makes matters worse, whether it's a statewide drought like California's, an illness in the family, or an impending layoff we face. The reality is that the situations in our lives and the world around us are constantly changing. If we don't respond to these changes in ways appropriate to the shifting circumstances, we'll overlook opportunities and may even aggravate the situation.

Obstacle to TR #2: Believing That Uncertainty Should Be Avoided

Japan, according to social science researchers, is a society that avoids uncertainty more than almost any other. It's no surprise, then, that Japanese students have begun to ask their professors to fail them so that they can repeat a year of university studies rather than graduate without having a job secured.[13]

The highly regimented Japanese system of obtaining jobs before graduation removes some of the uncertainty students face.

But educators and policymakers suggest that this risk avoidance behavior undermines students' education by diverting their energy from studying to extensive job searches. And, ironically, Japanese companies are beginning to hire more foreigners.

In some respects, the West shares this aversion to risk, despite the fact that uncertainty defined much of the twentieth century's successes. As cities became the center of American life, for example, citizens had to adjust from the rhythms of the farming season to the faster tempo of urban manufacturing. For millions, this radical shift was terrifying. People feared the future and what a job, a community, and even a family would look like.

But those who were able to face the "unknown" made immense progress with effects that last to this day. In the early 1900s Henry Ford, the son of farmers, convinced a group of businessmen to back him in a car-making enterprise amid a particularly unstable market and price fluctuations that led a number of companies to consolidate. He knew nothing about business, and his first attempts failed in part because of a falling-out with his investors. Rather than dwell on the uncertainty of these kinds of ventures and the volatility of the times, he built a second business. When the new business faced unexpected risks and rising costs, Ford didn't question his business acumen or the ambiguities of starting another venture. Instead, he gathered another group of investors to found the Ford Motor Company, one of the great American success stories—one of many in a century of unparalleled progress and uncertainty.

Obstacle to TR #3: Assuming There Is Only One Approach or Solution to a Given Problem

In the 1980s, scientists believed that stomach ulcers were caused by stress, spicy foods, and the buildup of stomach acids. They therefore ignored the findings of Australian physician Barry Marshall, who claimed that some ulcers were in fact caused by bacteria that lived in the stomach and that they could be cured with antibiotics. "You think, 'it's science; it's got to be accepted.' But it's not an absolute given. The idea was too weird," he recalled. Unable to shift the conventional thinking, Marshall came up with a novel way of approaching the problem. He concocted and drank a bacterial soup and actually gave himself an ulcer, proving that doctors had been asking the wrong questions for years and that the problem had to be approached in a totally different way to find a cure.

It took another ten years before the medical and scientific communities adapted to this new knowledge. But Marshall's discovery and his pursuit of new solutions and different ways of thinking led him to win the Nobel Prize. He is a reminder that we have to be creative in how we confront the challenges we face.[14] Narrowly focused approaches keep us from adapting, learning, and discovering important new solutions—all essential when the problems we face are novel. And many of today's problems at the community, business, and global levels are without precedent in scope and nature.

Obstacle to TR #4: Viewing Success as a Matter of Innate Talent

Dr. Marshall's story also points to the fact that some of our long-standing assumptions about success no longer serve us in this quickly changing world. We tend to think of successful people as those with innate talent and intelligence, often describing them as "brilliant," a "genius," or a "born leader." But research confirms that this assumption is a myth.

Harvard professor Howard Gardner found that IQ contributes to approximately only 20 percent of success in life; the rest depends on other capacities. Some of these factors have been investigated as far back as 1926, when psychologist Catharine Morris Cox studied three hundred established geniuses, from

Leonardo da Vinci to Charles Darwin and Albert Einstein, to discover which factors led to success or "realized genius" and those that might predict who would genuinely make a mark on the world. She found that a number of qualities beyond raw intelligence predicted "greatness."[15]

In 2007, building upon Cox's findings, University of Pennsylvania psychologist Angela Duckworth identified a set of characteristics she called "grit." Grit enables people to remain passionate and committed to a cause or project, to stay the course over long periods of time.

According to Duckworth, "Part of what it means to be gritty is to be resilient in the face of failure or adversity. Grit predicts success over and beyond talent. When you consider individuals of equal talent, the grittier ones do better."[16]

This overlaps with the unexpected discoveries Salvatore Maddi and his research team made in the 1980s when Illinois Bell Telephone unexpectedly cut its staff of twenty-six thousand in half. The researchers had been studying more than four hundred supervisors, managers, and executives when the layoffs occurred, so the scope of the study spans the time before, during, and after.

They found that two-thirds of the employees suffered significant performance, leadership, and health declines as a result of the upheaval. However, one-third actually thrived despite experiencing the same amount of disruption and stress as their coworkers. These workers had what Maddi called "hardiness," or a combination of attitudes that provides the commitment and self-control to successfully face stressful circumstances. As a result, these workers maintained their health, happiness, and performance and even felt renewed enthusiasm.[17]

The Way Is Forward

Truthfully, we're almost never the same person after we experience adversity or a stressful change. Often, the world we knew has shifted under our feet and there's no way to go back, even if we want to. Those who are able to reach within and summon Transformative Resilience will be those who don't just build a new life but also find ways to live more fully and successfully than before, drawing strength, new skills, and perspectives from challenge.

It's perhaps no coincidence that the year Dorothy and the Wizard of Oz were transported from written word to silver screen was the same year that World War II broke out. "There's no place like home, there's no place like home" was Dorothy's mantra. The idea of a pair of magic slippers that would transport her back to a simpler time appealed to those facing war and the growing uncertainty of the day.

Some have suggested that the original L. Frank Baum story reflected the distresses of the late-nineteenth-century financial crisis. Not knowing what shifting realities they would encounter at home and abroad, it's no wonder people felt the need to summon the heart, wisdom, and courage that the Tin Man, Scarecrow, and Cowardly Lion eventually found.

But what the movie delivered was a reminder that there was no Wizard of Oz who could solve Dorothy's problems or give her friends the abilities and strengths they desperately sought. Like Dorothy and her friends, we have to find our own capacity to overcome the impact of even the most unsettling experiences in our lives.

Life is never quite like the movies, as we know. We can't put on magic slippers that return us home to the safety of the known, the secure, the predictable—to a time or place that seems simpler or more manageable. We can't return to who we used to be, either. Trying to replicate what worked yesterday only makes us vulnerable.

In these turbulent times, we have to find a new definition of home. It's not a place so much as a mindset and an array of skills that give us a sense of belonging and shelter that we carry with us.

Perhaps what we truly long for is an expanded sense of self more suited to who we've become, what we value, and what works in the changing world around us.

Paradoxically, the foundation for this new "home" is the recognition that life is fundamentally unstable, uncontrollable, unpredictable, messy, and wonderfully surprising. We build upon this base with the knowledge that we can and must meet change head-on, that we can use stress and adversity to open the door to new opportunities. The certainty we seek is that we have the inner resources to transcend our challenges and in fact be transformed by them. When we find that security within, we can truly rest in the knowledge that there is no place like home.

CHAPTER 2

Transformative Resilience and the Adversity Sweet Spot

In the middle of difficulty lies opportunity.

Albert Einstein

On March 2, 2013, Stephanie Decker, a thirty-seven-year-old sleep specialist, marched into the halls of the Kentucky State Capitol to advocate for a bill requiring insurance companies to cover the costs for new and refurbished prosthetics. This particular march had extra significance: while other people start their day by putting on their shoes, Decker begins hers by putting on a pair of prosthetics that attach to her body just below her thighs. It's characteristic of her spirit, though, that she sees this as simply part of life; her day is no different from anybody else's. She just puts her legs on first.[1]

The year before, Decker had lost both her legs while protecting her children from a tornado that killed thirty-nine and left thousands homeless in a series of megastorms that raged across southern Indiana and Kentucky. As the vicious twister sped across the Deckers' fifteen acres, flattening everything in its path, she rushed her son Dominic, age eight, and her daughter Reese, age five, into the basement. The tornado, one in a pattern of increasingly devastating storms, devoured their three-story brick-and-stone house and then spit it back out in a heap.

When the storm cleared, Decker lay under a mountain of debris. Beneath her, her children, whom she had shielded with her body, were unscathed. But she quickly realized that both of her legs were badly hurt, and one was bleeding profusely.

Worrying for her children even amid her own injuries, she instructed Dominic to find a pair of mismatched flip-flops to put on his bare feet before running to get help. A neighbor, Chris Troncin, came to the rescue and got Reese out of the wreckage but was unable to remove Decker, forcing them to find further assistance. Waiting alone was difficult, especially once she realized the extent of her injuries and that her one leg had either been severed or was barely attached. Pelted by large hailstones and rain, she used her phone to record a farewell video to her husband and family, telling them how much she loved them. But there was no need for the message. After what seemed like a lifetime, she was evacuated to University of Louisville Hospital and rushed into surgery.

When she came out of the operating room, she asked her husband, Joe, "Did I lose my legs?"

"Yes," he whispered.

"I grieved for about ten minutes," she recalled. Then she told him, "We need a plan. We need to move forward. What are our options?"

"You're still in the ICU, Steph," Joe said.

"I'm ready to pick a direction. I need my life back," Decker responded.[2]

Four days after surgery, she joked with reporters from her hospital wheelchair. Just two months later, after countless grueling physical therapy sessions, she stood on her first prosthetic legs and began to learn to walk again. In the months following the accident, Decker and her husband founded the Stephanie Decker Foundation, which helps children with prosthetics get involved in sports. "So many good things have come from this accident," Decker reflected. "I know that's kind of strange to say. But now it's our turn to serve others."[3]

One and a half weeks shy of the first anniversary of the tornado, the Kentucky House honored Decker for single-handedly putting "prosthetic parity" on lawmakers' radar and for pushing for equal care for amputees from state to state. She used the opportunity to make a plea for those who had lost limbs. In her appeal to the members of the House Committee on Banking and Insurance, she said, "Help me help kids walk and play," her voice breaking with emotion. "You don't think it's going to be you. I didn't think it was going to be me." Her impassioned advocacy paid off and the bill was passed.

Stephanie Decker took charge of a situation that would have defeated many of us and turned it into a positive. She attributes this in part to being "hardwired" for optimism and finding the best in every situation. But she's also aware that she's setting an example for her children and wants them to understand everyone struggles and everyone has a story. "It's how you deal with your story that makes the difference in your life," she explained.

Walking tires her. She can spend four or five hours on her prostheses, which is approximately equivalent to sixteen hours on one's own legs. But she is deeply grateful. "When I get to wake up and see my kids every day, it squashes that 'Man, this is hard' [mindset] really quick." If anything, she said, "this has given us our purpose."

* * *

Few of us have been prepared to deal with the level of unpredictability and volatility present in our turbulent world. Stephanie Decker's story is a prime example of the fact that how we respond to what happens has the greatest influence on the course of our personal and professional lives and on the outcomes of local and global challenges. She not only handled adversity and stress but also grew as a result. People like Decker point to the human capacity for Transformative Resilience and the Type R mindset and skills.

All around us, whether in nature or in the man-made world, a resounding number of examples remind us that growth from adversity is possible and it is not a rare exception; in some respects, it may even be the norm. To be successful, individuals, leaders, organizations, and even families must integrate the challenges they've experienced and accept—even embrace—uncertainty, with the recognition that knowledge, innovation, and progress are often born from change and challenges. Much of this depends on the way that we individually or collectively frame adversity, the stories we tell ourselves, and whether we can find opportunity in challenges, stress, and disruptive change.

Growth under Pressure

The novelist Haruki Murakami eloquently described the evolution people go through in the face of turbulence. "And once the storm is over, you won't remember how you made it through, how you managed to survive," he wrote. "But one thing is certain. When you come out of the storm, you won't be the same person who walked in. That's what this storm's all about."[4]

We've long seen this phenomenon in the natural world, where there are signs of growth and evolution from adversity all around us. Fire is the mechanism by which many forests are repeatedly regenerated, according to NASA's earth scientists. The lodgepole pine can't release its seeds without the intense heat fires provide. Carbon is transformed into diamonds only as a result of heat and pressure. And researchers increasingly find that, although it takes different forms, we as humans are also transformed and grow under pressure from our environments.

It's then no surprise that the origin stories of superheroes incorporate momentous, unforeseen, and often alarming events that radically alter their lives. The Flash was struck by lightning and bathed in electrically charged chemicals, giving him super speed to fight crime and rescue others; Barbara Gordon's transformation into Batgirl was catalyzed by an encounter with Batman and the ongoing stress of abuse she suffered after her mother's death plunged her father into drinking. Is it possible that these situations are closer to reality than we could have imagined?

People often emerge from excessive stress, ongoing pressures, and difficult experiences with a perspective that allows them to recognize opportunities where they might never have seen them before. These people convert hardship into personal achievement and are compelled to participate in the larger world. Though these individuals are *not* superheroes, they do embody an important kind of strength—Transformative Resilience.

The positive effects of struggling with stressful and traumatic events have been prominent themes throughout human history. The idea that suffering and distress can potentially yield positive change is thousands of years old. It can be found in the writings of the ancient Hebrews, Greeks, and early Christians as well in the teachings of Hinduism and Buddhism. They all address the potential for transformative growth from adversity.

In the early 1980s, Lawrence Calhoun and Richard Tedeschi began research at the University of North Carolina that led to the now widely accepted phenomenon of post-traumatic growth (PTG). This concept was based on interviews with widows, people who had been disabled through accidents or illness, and people who had experienced traumatic events in the military. Calhoun and Tedeschi discovered that, although these situations did cause suffering, the suffering was not the end point. They found that up to 60 percent of people who experienced a severely traumatic event underwent a period of growth.[5] For many, their pain became a catalyst that spurred the survivors to find greater meaning in their lives.[6]

People who experience PTG report a certain amount of positive change in their external lives, but the majority of the growth is often internal. They report that their lives have improved; however, externally their lives frequently don't appear significantly different from before the traumatic event.

The stresses and adversity that most of us face go beyond a single traumatic event. They can also come in the form of gradual, mounting pressures, ongoing change, and constant uncertainty. The shift toward TR signals a monumental change in thinking and harnesses the idea emerging among a number of academics, researchers, and businesspeople that resilience must include an element of evolution and growth.

TR focuses on strength and ingenuity, whether in individuals or groups, leaders, families, or businesses. It also prepares us for reality that now that chaotic disruption is the new normal, there's no longer a status quo, only the ongoing process of change.

Adversity Is a Terrible Thing to Waste

There is a story of a man who had a horse that ran away. When his neighbor found out, he said, "That's terrible." The man said, "You never know." The next day the horse came back and was leading two wild horses. The neighbor said, "That's wonderful." The man said, "You never know." His only son was training one of the wild horses and fell off and broke his leg. The neighbor said, "That's terrible." The man said, "You never know." The Cossack army came through the village and recruited all the young men except the son because he had a broken leg. Again the neighbor said, "That's wonderful." And again the man said, "You never know." And it goes on and on. We make all kinds of assumptions in life. But the truth is that many of our assumptions prove incorrect.

Most of us assume that if a situation is painful, difficult, or unpleasant, it's bad, when in fact it is often an unforeseen blessing. Although none of us would ever choose to experience adversity, many of the most content, healthiest people are those who have had some early ordeals.

In the nursery business there is a tried-and-true process for starting young plants called hardening off. Every spring before the seedlings are transplanted, the tender young plants are taken out of the greenhouse and put under protective cover. There, they are gradually exposed to more extreme temperatures—not enough to freeze them, but just enough to toughen them up. The nursery staff also limits water, to create thicker stems, and occasionally the plants are even deprived of nutrients for a particular period of time. Through this process of deprivation, the tiny plants become stronger and finally strong enough to survive all the adverse conditions they will face in the garden. No one's saying we should deprive anyone of food or water, regardless of how naughty they've been. But plants go through a process parallel to that of people exposed to stress. As a result of the struggle, plants grow bigger and stronger, their root systems deepen and expand. If they are not hardened off, the chance they will reach their full potential decreases considerably.

Recent studies suggest that resilience and related growth may have at least as much to do with how often people have faced adversity in the past as with who they are—their personality, their genes—or what they are currently facing. That is, the number of blows people take during their lifetime may affect their mental and physical toughness more than any other factor.

Mark Seery, a researcher in the Department of Psychology at the University at Buffalo, and his colleagues have surveyed and monitored the mental well-being of thousands of adults ranging in age from 18 to 101 years. They track the number and kind of difficult experiences these people have had, including divorce, the death of a friend or parent, financial setbacks, serious illness, and being in a natural disaster.[7]

"There is this middle sweet spot," Seery says when we speak with him. "You need to be exposed to some difficulties that may be unpleasant in the moment, and later on you get this benefit . . . and [ability to] cope better with subsequent stressors."[8]

Seery explains that this toughening carries over from one source to another. In other words, someone like Stephanie Decker who has lived through a natural disaster will have experienced a toughening that carries across contexts into new stressful, trying, or even changing circumstances.

Seery likens this to physical fitness. To develop fitness, you need to exercise, you need to place that initial stress on your body. He's also quick to point out that you can overwork or overstress your body and cause damage, leading to negative effects. However, if you never work out at all, you never have the opportunity to develop fitness.

He goes a step further and confirms that this toughening is an important evolution. "This can absolutely be [seen] as a form of growth after experiencing adversity," Seery explains. He adds that you can also experience this growth and Transformative Resilience from more mundane challenges and other types of stresses. It isn't just trauma and large stressors that help us expand our abilities.

Enduring hardship and weathering change also build a sense of confidence. This is true not only for individuals but also for people in leadership roles and for groups of people, whether businesses, classes of students, or families that together undergo, confront, and grow from challenging times. It may be that experience with a moderate number of hardships strengthens a belief in ourselves or in a group of which we are a part and in our ability to think through and cope with the challenges life, work, and the world present to us.

And, as we discuss in Chapter 4, further research shows that there are ways to level the playing field so that regardless of the number of challenges we've faced, we can have equally positive responses, experience Transformative Resilience, and spring forward.

The Stories We Tell Ourselves

On a day back in 2007, commuters hurried by without realizing that the unassuming young man in a baseball cap and jeans, busking in a Washington, DC, Metro stop, was none other than the virtuoso Grammy-winning violinist Joshua Bell. Bell normally plays to sold-out audiences who pay hundreds of dollars to see him perform. However, *Washington Post* columnist Gene Weingarten had asked Bell to participate in an experiment. He wanted to see how people would respond if Bell performed in a different setting, changing the context in which people saw him.[9]

Among the 1,097 people who witnessed Bell play that day, only seven stopped to listen, despite the fact that he was performing exactly the same pieces he plays on stage. In this new and unexpected context, the commuters didn't see him in the same way that they did when they experienced his playing in a theater.

We assume that we look at situations through the best, correct, or only set of lenses, but being able to question and shift our frame of reference—to look at situations from different viewpoints—is essential when we confront challenges in a constantly changing world.

Our capacity for Transformative Resilience, to a great extent, depends on the stories we tell ourselves, whether as individuals or collectively as members of families, organizations, or national cultures. What happens to us matters far less than the way we interpret the situation. We continually create frames for what we see and experience that both inform and limit the way we think.

Telling ourselves a negative story not only affects the way we view the situation but also can impair our ability to cope. Conversely, a more positive framing better enables us to see possibilities and opportunities in difficult circumstances and to take the necessary action to move forward.

In 2013, Steven M. Southwick, Yale University's post-traumatic stress expert, hosted an interdisciplinary dialogue among a group of eminent experts across science, sociology, and psychology about their approaches to dealing with stress and trauma. Simply put, the focus is moving away from what's wrong with people toward what is right and what is working well. Across the disciplines, the various experts had begun to ask "What are the mechanisms that allow most people to cope so well?" But this framing stretches even further. The group, which included an anthropologist and psychiatrists and medical experts, investigated resilience in different contexts. They observed that the common theme is the need to look at an entire system to see what allows it to adapt to the disruptions that threaten its ability to function well and continue to develop, whether that system is contained within an individual, a business, a family, or a community.[10]

For example, two people facing extraordinary but similar situations fashion drastically different narratives about them, and those narratives color their lives and their futures. If you lose your job, do you see it as a personal punishment that shames you, exposing your weaknesses and failure? Or do you see it as a common story, affected by larger forces—say, the export of hundreds of thousands of jobs—and therefore recognize that larger global trends have acted on your situation? Either way, losing a job is difficult, but one story propels a person into despair, the other, into possibility and finding new ways of operating in a changing world. How we shape our stories shapes our lives. Reframing involves changing your perspective on a given situation to give it a more positive or beneficial meaning.

James W. Pennebaker at the University of Texas asked healthy college students to write about the most emotionally charged experience of their lives for four consecutive days for fifteen minutes each day. The study participants who gained the most from the exercise were trying to make meaning of the distress. They examined the causes and outcomes of the hardship and, as a result, became more insightful and knowledgeable about it.

In fact, their stories helped them discover opportunity in their adversity. And, when people opened up privately about a stressful life event, they were more likely to talk with others about it. This suggests that telling one's story leads indirectly to reaching out for social support that can aid in the healing process and cultivate a shared healthy mindset.

During the six months following the experiment, the people who made meaning of their experiences visited the campus health center less often and used pain relievers less frequently than those who wrote about insignificant matters.[11]

The stories we tell ourselves shape how we think, what we believe, the choices we make, and the actions we take. Of equal importance are the stories we collectively tell ourselves as families, groups of coworkers, businesses, communities, and countries.

For instance, in the wake of multiple bombings of London's public transportation system in 2005, UK leaders, media, and public discussion largely focused on framing the story as one of a people with a long history of overcoming adversity and thus who were able to overcome it again.

While the London Underground protected people from bombs in World War II, it was now a place where bombs were exploding. And yet the overwhelming story was one of resilience, urging the British people to stay strong. "London can take it" and similar headlines emblazoned newspapers and blogs of the United Kingdom and its allies, like the United States. In her commemorative address following the July 7 bombings, the Queen called on the country's past and the memory of those who had faced World War II to tell a story of a collective identity and embodiment of resilience, sustained courage, and humor.[12]

Reframing Adversity

Mounting stress, failure, and change are far more common in our lives than the traumatic events that dramatically change things from one moment to the next. If we can take even the most appalling experiences and grow from them, we can also use the increasing pressures and challenges of everyday life to our advantage, as long as we are able to reframe them. When we change the frame, we radically change the breadth of likely solutions.

Research shows that the "event" aspect of our lives accounts for less than 8 to 15 percent of the changes in our life satisfaction.[13] That means that 85 to 92 percent of how content we are, how we deal with challenges and setbacks, and our overall sense of well-being is attributable to the meaning we make of what happens to us in everyday life. In other words, we have a conscious ability to choose how we perceive roughly 85 to 92 percent of the events in our lives.

Take, for example, earthquakes in China. For decades they have been an ever-present stressor in the lives of the Chinese people that intensify only during specific periods. In 2008 a series of eight earthquakes shook Sichuan Province. More than half of the two thousand survivors reported having experienced positive growth in the aftermath. They believed they had developed personal strength, a sense of appreciation for life, or an openness to new opportunities.[14]

Each time stresses from the natural environment flare up, from devastating floods to tornadoes, or acts of terrorism and violence converge, interviews with survivors are rich with positive outlooks. The common theme echoed in the wake of difficult circumstances is that the experience "brought our community closer" and is "a reminder of what is really important in life." Individuals who frequently use reframing to change their emotional response to stress and adversity report greater psychological well-being and more positive outcomes and growth compared to individuals who do not use positive reframing as a coping style.[15]

Four years after her own experience with natural disaster, Stephanie Decker shared a renewed respect for nature and gratitude for life. "Never forget how powerful Mother Nature can be, never forget how our time on this earth is not decided by us and to cherish every damn minute of it because there is no promise of a tomorrow. [And], never get too busy in your lives to stop what you're doing and just LIVE for the moment," she urged.

The Advantages of Stress (Yes, Really)

It has long been recognized that stress is detrimental to our health. It's blamed for a multitude of illnesses ranging from the common cold to heart disease. However, how we perceive stress can be just as important as the amount of stress we're experiencing.

A Harvard study tracked thirty thousand adults in the United States over a period of eight years, from 1998 to 2006. It began by asking the participants, "How much stress have you experienced in the last year?" and "Do you believe that stress is harmful for your health?" Then the researchers tracked deaths and causes.[16]

As expected, people who had experienced a lot of stress in the previous year showed a 43 percent increased risk of dying—but this wasn't true for everyone. Participants who didn't view stress as harmful were not more likely to die. In fact, they had the lowest risk of dying of anyone in the study, including people who experienced very little stress. Researchers concluded that the belief that stress is bad in many respects makes it detrimental.

In a 2013 follow-up study at Harvard University, participants who were told that the physiological signs of stress prepared them to cope better became less anxious and more confident in stressful situations. They viewed their stress response as helpful. As a result, their hearts and blood vessels responded to stress in the same manner that they would in times of intense happiness.[17]

The new science of stress suggests that it may be how we think about stress that matters. Though it's clear that not all stresses are the same.

For many of the day-to-day pressures that we face, we might do well to shift our focus from eliminating them to changing our perception of them and asking different questions. We might instead ask, How can I use the energy created by this stress to help me better cope with the challenge I am facing? or What can I learn from this stress and how does it help me change and grow?

The Harvard study shows that if we view our stress response as beneficial to our functioning, we'll be less anxious, less stressed, and more focused and self-assured. When we stop trying to avoid it, stress can actually energize us.

Moderate, short-lived stress can improve alertness and performance and boost memory. The stress hormone cortisol is released when people are put under pressure. If released in moderate amounts, it triggers increased learning and memory.

Studies have also shown that stress may increase the production of another hormone, oxytocin, also referred to as the "trust hormone." Oxytocin can help alleviate social anxiety and increases empathy and connection with others. This, in turn, can buffer us from the effects of high cortisol levels, which can be detrimental to our health, by enabling us to turn stressful situations into opportunities to reach out and build deeper connections with others.[18]

However, some stresses can be detrimental if they are not addressed, such as prolonged illness, lengthy periods of unemployment, or ongoing marital strife, to name a few. And we have to be aware that stress associated with situations like lifelong poverty and racial and gender discrimination may have different impacts than those currently being studied by researchers at Harvard and elsewhere.

What amounts to too much stress differs for each of us, so we need to be sensitive to the early warning symptoms and signs that suggest a stress overload is starting to push us over the edge. Such signals also differ for each of us and can be so subtle that they are often ignored until it is too late. The key to using stress to our advantage is knowing ourselves and understanding that there's a threshold for each of us beyond which stress is no longer productive. In part, this means taking time to regularly reflect on our mental and physical state, drawing on our past experiences and feedback from those who know us well, whether friends, family, or colleagues.

Failing Forward

Failure or the prospect of it is one of the greatest sources of stress and challenge that we face throughout our lives. How we approach failure is critical to Transformative Resilience as well as our core sense of who we are. Kathryn Schulz, author of *Being Wrong,* remarked on the human benefit of failure when she wrote, "And far from being a mark of indifference or intolerance, wrongness is a vital part of how we learn and change. Thanks to error, we can revise our understanding of ourselves and amend our ideas about the world."[19]

For many people in our success-driven culture, failure isn't just considered a non-option—it's considered a deficiency. Yet, when we look back at some of the seminal figures in history, a willingness to risk failure isn't a new or unusual concept. Charles Darwin was considered a failure at school and university, yet he went on to become one of the most famous and influential scientists of the nineteenth century. Walt Disney was fired from the *Kansas City Star* for "lacking imagination," and his first attempt at business ended in bankruptcy, but he went on to found the world's most famous animation studio. After winning the international bid, world-renowned architect Zaha Hadid had her design for the Cardiff Bay Opera House in the United Kingdom rejected; however, she went on to use the same design to build the critically acclaimed Guangzhou Opera House in China, and in 2004 she became the first woman to win the Pritzker Architecture Prize, the most prestigious award in the field. Failure is often an essential tool in growth, learning, Transformative Resilience, and achieving success.

Thomas Edison is a particularly inspiring historical example of the idea of failing forward. In West Orange, New Jersey, in the early evening of December 9, 1914, a massive fire erupted in Edison's laboratory. Fire departments from eight surrounding towns rushed to the scene, but the chemical-fueled firestorm was impossible to extinguish quickly. Much of Edison's life's work went up in the spectacular blaze. Edison lost approximately $919,788—the equivalent of about $23 million today.

At the height of the fire, Edison's twenty-four-year-old son, Charles, frantically searched for his father in the smoke and debris. He finally found him calmly watching the scene, his face glowing in the reflection.

"My heart ached for him," said Charles. "He was sixty-seven—no longer a young man—and everything was going up in flames." But to his surprise, the next morning Edison looked at the ruins and said, "There is great value in disaster. All our mistakes are burned up. Thank God we can start anew."

Like many of today's younger people, Edison was an entrepreneur. In fact, he was one of America's earliest serial entrepreneurs, if not the first.[20] He was willing to take risks, continually learn from his mistakes, and persevere despite a multitude of failures. However, today, our culture rarely sees failure and adversity as beneficial, particularly if they don't ultimately lead to a success story. In fact, many of us avoid the prospect of failure and when it finds its way to our door we look to return to the point from which we've come—to rebuild in the mold of what has been before rather than what is yet to come.

Consider how Steve Jobs famously reframed his firing from Apple. In his Stanford University graduation address, he noted, "I didn't see it then, but it turned out that getting fired from Apple was the best thing that could have ever happened to me. . . . It freed me to enter one of the most creative periods of my life. . . . I'm pretty sure none of this would have happened if I hadn't been fired." Equally, J. K. Rowling, one of the world's most successful writers, talks about how failure allowed her to re-evaluate in critical ways. She found that she was freed by failure because her greatest fears had already come to pass. She could now stop trying to live up to other people's expectations and direct all of her energy into finishing her novels, the thing that mattered most to her.

A study published in *Psychological Science* expands on the concept that wisdom can be wrung from failure. Jason Moser and his colleagues at Michigan State University examined the convergence of psychology and physiology. The researchers discovered that people who believe they can learn from mistakes and mishaps have a different level of brain activity than those who believe they cannot. The question at the center of the research is straightforward: Why are some people more effective at learning from their slip-ups? After all, we all make them. The essential part is what we do next. Do we ignore the mistake, or do we explore the error, determined to learn from it?[21]

While measuring subjects' brain activity using an electroencephalograph, Moser and his colleagues gave the participants a simple chore to do in which it was easy to slip up. Subjects were asked to identify the middle letter of a five-letter series, such as "MMMMM" or "NNMNN." Sometimes the middle letter was the same as the other four, and sometimes it was different. "It's pretty simple doing the same thing over and over again, but the mind can't help it; it just kind of zones out from time to time." This simple change induced frequent mistakes. When subjects made an error, they noticed it immediately.

When a person erred, the researchers observed two rapid signals on the EEG: an initial response that indicated something had gone wrong—Moser called it the "Oh, crap" response—and a second signal that indicated the individual was aware of the error and was trying to understand what went wrong. Both signals happened within a quarter of a second of the mistake.

Once the experiment was completed, the researchers asked the subjects if they believed they could learn from missteps. The participants who believed they could learn from their mistakes had done better after making one—in other words, they successfully recovered after an error. Their brains also reacted differently, producing a larger second signal, the one that indicates, "I see that I've made a mistake, and I will learn from it."

Failures continually test us and distinguish those of us who can make positive meaning from setbacks and those who are either unwilling or unable to use hardship to their advantage.

The Power of Positive Emotions

In a famous Native American story, an old Cherokee tells his grandson that inside all people a battle rages between two wolves. One wolf is negativity: anger, sadness, stress, envy, greed, fear, arrogance, guilt, shame, and hate. The other is positivity: joy, gratitude, hope, compassion, faith, and, above all, love. The grandson thinks about this for a moment, then asks, "Well, which wolf wins?" The grandfather replies, "The one you feed."

Transformative Resilience isn't about glossing over the negative emotions associated with failure, stress, loss, and change in our lives but instead is about letting them sit side by side with other feelings. "I'm really sad about that," a resilient person may think, "but I'm also grateful about this." People with a more positive outlook are more likely to experience TR because they see opportunities that negative people don't.

One of the most renowned studies on positive emotions demonstrates that they don't just make us feel good but may actually prolong our lives. Researchers reviewed the diaries of 180 nuns from the School Sisters of Notre Dame, all born before 1917, who had chronicled their thoughts in autobiographical journal entries. More than fifty years later, psychologists who came across this treasure trove of information codified the entries and correlated them with the outcomes of the writers' lives. The most overtly joyful lived nearly ten years longer than the nuns whose entries were more negative or neutral. By age eighty-five, 90 percent of the happiest nuns were still alive compared to just 34 percent of the others.[22]

Positive emotions change the way our minds and bodies work, including the way our cells change and are renewed; indeed, they alter the very nature of who we are, influencing our outlook on life and our ability to confront disruptive change and challenges.[23]

Individuals who embrace TR are more adept at springing forward because they are emotionally complex. They don't deceive themselves with positivity; rather, these individuals look for something redeeming in the midst of difficult situations. They shift their focus to a positive outlook more rapidly and they respond to adversity by drawing on a broader range of emotions.

In a study of the relationship between negative and positive emotions, psychologists Jack Bauer and George Bonanno interviewed people six months after they had lost a spouse. The researchers tracked both the positive and negative comments the respondents made about the lost relationship, then conducted a follow-up interview two years later. The people who were coping most successfully were the ones who had made roughly five positive comments to each negative one. People who were more negative were not doing as well—and neither were those who had made only positive comments. The ones who adjusted the best were those who could acknowledge the sadness of their situation without being overwhelmed by it.[24]

Why are positive emotions so important? Because, according to researchers, they can provide a surefire remedy for stress and worry. They undo the negative impacts of a difficult experience.[25]

Alfred Hitchcock, the master of suspense, once said, "There is no terror in a bang, only in the anticipation of it." Hitchcock touched on a subject that has long interested researchers: that awaiting a stressful event is itself stressful.

In another study, Barbara Fredrickson, a professor of psychology at the University of North Carolina, and her colleagues asked subjects to wear a heart rate monitor. Once participants' baseline heart rate was recorded, the researchers gave participants just one minute to prepare a speech on "why you are a good friend" and told them that their presentation would be videotaped and evaluated by their peers. Participants' heart rates were measured again, and researchers found that rates had increased dramatically for most participants. Their arteries had constricted and their blood pressure soared.[26]

Next, participants were told that if they viewed a film clip they didn't have to give the speech. Subjects were then shown a clip of tranquil ocean waves, a snippet of a puppy playing, a scene from a sad film, or a screen saver depicting an abstract display of lines. These images were meant to arouse negative emotions such as sadness, positive emotions such as contentment and joy, or no emotional response.

As the film started, participants' apprehension began to diminish. Sensors tracking heart rate, blood pressure, and artery constriction showed that subjects who watched the positive imagery recovered from their distress the fastest, far more quickly than those who viewed the negative and neutral film clips. The researchers concluded that positive emotions can reverse the effects of a stressful situation. They further discovered that the people with the greatest resilience were also more positive in their everyday lives.

Not surprisingly, people who cultivate TR are better at converting negative emotions into positive ones. One of the most significant discoveries of Fredrickson's research is that resilient people had a different approach to the speech challenge than that of their nonresilient counterparts. They saw the assignment as a challenge, an opportunity for learning and development, rather than as a test. They used the challenge to their advantage. Resilient people are good at recovering because they have a multifaceted approach to emotions. They respond to adversity by embracing a broad array of feelings.

Positive emotions are key to helping people deal with adversity and live a meaningful life. They open us. They change the limits of our minds and our attitude toward our world and our future.

The way that we approach failure, hardship, and setbacks has a significant effect on how we cope with change and adversity. Although we may not be able to control our external circumstances, one of the magnificent things about human beings is that we can *always* choose our attitudes. It's essential not to deny a challenging situation, but we must look for a redeeming quality in the midst of difficulty—view our failures, losses, and challenges as learning opportunities and be open to new experiences.

Granted, it's unlikely that any of us who have lived through adversity, disruptive change, or inordinate stress would ever seek it out or choose to relive such experiences, but if we can adopt a Type R mindset and recognize that tough times change us for the better, we can grow in important and meaningful ways. Type R provides the framework and skills that enable us to use adversity, change, and life's challenges as opportunities for innovation, creativity, growth, and transformation.

CHAPTER 3

Type R: The Mindset for Our Time

There is nothing either good or bad,
but thinking makes it so.

William Shakespeare

IN 1982 JONATHAN Blake was one of the first people in the United Kingdom to be diagnosed with HIV. "In those days it was a death sentence," says Jonathan, now in his sixties, when we sit with him in his South London apartment. "It was very difficult, because I had this killer virus coursing through my veins, I didn't want to pass it to anyone, and I was feeling very isolated. It was a wretched time. Essentially I felt like a leper."[1]

In December of that year, Jonathan hit an all-time low and considered whether it was worth living. But thinking about his loved ones kept him strong. He made it through that time and ultimately decided, "You've got to get out and live. But that's easier said than done because my self-confidence was zilch—[I thought to myself,] 'Who is going to want to know me?' . . . I suppose that I had essentially hidden myself away to protect myself. But I had to find a way to get out of that rut."

He read an article about a protest that was being organized by the gay community. Although he was apprehensive about going, Jonathan figured "this will be my re-entry into society." When he got to the meeting place, he struck up a conversation with a good-looking man named Nigel. Jonathan remembers he had a full head of black, curly hair and was wearing Wellington boots and a pair of bright crimson pants. They spent the entire day together and into the evening, when they decided to go to a party. That day signaled a major shift for Jonathan as well as the start of an incredibly fulfilling relationship that has now spanned over thirty years.

"I knew I was going to be dead next week—HIV was terminal," Jonathan says, "so I thought, 'What have I got to lose?'" He moved in with Nigel and started pursuing a degree in tailoring. "Your whole mindset changes in those terms. So I thought, 'Why not do things differently?'"

But Jonathan couldn't have imagined the life-changing opportunities that would emerge through his renewed willingness to engage in life. As increasingly active members of the gay and lesbian community, Jonathan and Nigel, with the support of local authorities, helped found a gay and lesbian housing cooperative, where they live to this day.

That community became an anchor for Jonathan and a way to further invest in life. "Having come from nothing [and feeling] that one's life was completely closed down . . . suddenly there were all sorts of openings. Once you have a roof over your head you can do anything," he says.

In 1984, Jonathan and Nigel also became involved with a London-based group of gays and lesbians supporting miners striking against Margaret Thatcher's government, which had decided to close mines across the nation, dramatically affecting working-class communities built around the coal industry.

"When you see a community like the miners and what they had and you see it being destroyed and know that it's important, you want to help," Jonathan explains. "And because of being gay—the law had always been against us. We understood what they must feel, so there was this extraordinary common cause. At first [the miners] didn't get it. But once we met them and started to talk together, it was extraordinary. They understood where we were coming from . . . they welcomed us into their homes and they couldn't do enough for us."

Despite the fact that many mines were eventually closed, the National Union of Mineworkers continued to honor the alliances made with the LGBT community and years later was instrumental in helping British LGBT citizens gain the rights they enjoy today.

Growing up, Jonathan had a strong sense of family and community that contributes to the positive outlook that has helped him cope with his HIV and has enabled him to take on challenges in the world around him, like those faced by the mining community. "I guess that it was always inside of me. . . . Somehow I think that I was brought up [believing] that however dark things are, I can always find something positive."

Jonathan turned what could have been the worst news of his life into opportunity and a lifetime of significance. In many respects his ability to reframe his illness allowed him to take advantage of life and engage. "It gave me permission to let go and just see the way that things go," he says.

However, part of it was ensuring there were bright spots in his life as a way of coping. He always made sure to have something to look forward to, like theater tickets or a night at the opera, believing that that also mentally takes you forward. This holds true for any of us who are wrestling with a challenge. To the extent possible, it's important to structure our time so that there's always something on the horizon to look forward to.

Although Jonathan's health isn't perfect, he has successfully lived with HIV for over thirty-five years. "I feel grateful every day. The funny thing is that this life I've had with HIV, I wouldn't have missed it for the world. It's taken me on some amazing adventures."

✲ ✲ ✲

People like Jonathan Blake point to the vastly different responses people can have to adversity. This raises a question: What makes some so capable of thriving despite challenge and in some cases specifically because of it?

Increasingly, research indicates that mindset is one of the most critical factors. Our mindset is the filter through which we see everything, both as individuals and collectively. It comprises our assumptions, beliefs, and expectations, and it guides our actions. Mindset frames the ongoing monologue that takes place in our heads. It's the attitude that shapes our thoughts and how we perceive and respond to events.

Our mindset informs how we react to adversity, from the emotions we experience to how we cope with a situation. It significantly influences whether we thrive in the face of challenge or succumb to depression and despair. And emerging research consistently demonstrates that *what we believe* about our potential for change influences how we frame things, what motivates us, and ultimately how resilient we are. Shifting the way we think about stressful life events, change, and crisis can transform everyday hassles as well as how we approach and relate to life's significant challenges and shocks. We convince ourselves that our interpretation of circumstances and events is accurate because it's framed through an overarching attitude that is so pervasive it shapes all aspects of our lives.

Jonathan had a strong sense of family and community that gave him a head start. But no matter where we are in terms of our current level of Transformative Resilience, it's *always* possible to increase our capacity. We can develop the behaviors that support TR throughout our lifetime.

The fact is, we create our personal version of reality. That's why two people or even two teams can experience the exact same situation and come away with completely different impressions of what's occurred. The paradox of a mindset is that we often don't even realize that we have one until we gain some perspective or adopt a new one.

If our core beliefs don't support us, then frequently, whenever we're confronted with a challenging situation or obstacle, we give up and retreat into helplessness and defeat, when in fact what may be required is greater effort, more resources, deeper support, or a different approach to the situation. However, what's essential to using life's challenges as opportunities is a supportive attitude.

Mindset Equals Reality

On a fall day in 1981, a group of men in their seventies stepped into a time warp. From the moment they walked through the doors of a converted monastery in Peterborough, New Hampshire, they were treated as if they were twenty-two years younger. Perry Como and Nat "King" Cole crooned on a classic radio. *Ed Sullivan* was playing on a black-and-white TV. The entire space was filled with memorabilia from 1959. In fact, everything was impeccably designed to lead the men to experience their world from the perspective of their younger selves. This was their new home for the week as they participated in Harvard psychologist Ellen Langer's radical Counterclockwise study.

Langer and her colleagues set up the experiment to prove that our mindsets and the way we view ourselves have direct impacts on our physical realities and the aging process. The researchers created the same altered reality for two separate groups, which each spent a week living in the past. However, the experimental group was instructed not to just reminisce about these earlier years but also to attempt to *be* the person they were twenty-two years before. In comparison, the control group lived in the same replicated world, except they were told to stay in the present and simply reminisce about the earlier era.

Before arriving, the men had been assessed on every aspect of their lives that we assume deteriorates with age—dexterity, strength, flexibility, hearing and vision, memory and cognition. After each weeklong retreat, the researchers retested all the participants and found that, indeed, the mind has enormous control over the body.

There were dramatic positive changes across the board. The experimental group—the group instructed to "become" their younger selves—showed greater improvements on many measures of physical ability, health, and intelligence. They showed greater improvement in joint flexibility and performance on memory tests. Their average eyesight improved 10 percent. And, in intelligence tests, 63 percent of the experimental group improved their scores compared to only 44 percent of the control group.

Langer concluded, "The experimental subjects had put their minds in an earlier time and their bodies went along for the ride." She challenged everything that was thought to be the basis for physiology, functioning, and aging and demonstrated the dramatic role our mindsets play in determining our behaviors, physical well-being, and influence on reality.[2]

We have a greater ability to shape our own emotional, intellectual, and physical lives than most people realize, Langer explains during a conversation with us. "People don't realize that outcomes are in our heads. They're not in events," she says.[3]

At the end of the Counterclockwise study, Langer was able to conclude that it's not our physical selves that most limit us but rather our set of beliefs about ourselves and about the world. "It is our mindset about our own limits, our perceptions, that draws the lines in the sand," she wrote.

Langer's study reveals that our external reality is much more supple than most of us think. She proved that both individual as well as collective attitudes alter our reality.

The Mindset for Our Time

Jonathan Blake and the older adults in Langer's experiment were able to alter their realities through the power of the mind. They demonstrate that adopting an appropriate mindset can significantly influence how we approach adversity and thus the outcome.

This points to the ways in which our perceptions and mindsets frame how we interpret the experiences, events, and challenges we encounter in our lives and the world around us. Are we confined by what has come before and the circumstances we confront or can we continue to evolve and grow?

What we call the Type R mindset and accompanying skills, behaviors, and modes of operating are the underpinnings of Transformative Resilience. The Type R mindset provides a structure through which we view our own abilities, particularly in the face of change, challenge, and stressful life events. Those who have a Type R mindset—we call them Type Rs—view adversity not as a setback but as an opportunity for transformation and growth.

The growth at the heart of this is enabled by the Type R core belief that wherever we are in our lives we always have the ability to learn more, become more capable, adapt to our circumstances, and grow in the face of challenge. This holds true for individuals, leaders, organizations, and even whole families.

The Type R mindset has less to do with demographics and more to do with psychographics—core values and beliefs. Type Rs don't let adversity define them. They transcend, recognizing that difficult times are a temporary state of affairs.

Although they don't enjoy failure and hardship, they believe that these can serve as the foundation for insight and innovation and as vital sources of information for future success. Type Rs use adversity to ignite their strengths with the knowledge that they have the resources necessary to meet the challenges they face. They look for opportunities that might be by-products of their setbacks or stressful and painful experiences.

Regardless of our age or background, if we think of ourselves as adaptable, confident, robust, and able to continue to grow, we will spring forward from the stress and challenges in our lives. If we think of ourselves as frightened and unable to change, that, too, will become a reality. Our individual and collective mindsets will make it so.

The Type R mindset and accompanying skills and vision are the shock absorber that enables people and organizations to cope with the day-to-day stresses as well as the seismic events. It equips them to thrive in an increasingly volatile world, providing a vehicle for navigating the demanding times in which we live and work.

Consider the unprecedented change and the numerous challenges of the past decades that so many of us are struggling to accept, reframe, and learn from. Over a number of years, American prosperity has declined and an era of ultraconnectivity, digitalization, and globalization has been ushered in. The face of relationships and families has changed many times over, from increasing divorce rates to changing demographics and the spread of HIV, to name a few. We have been shaped by a string of wars in the Middle East and shocking events such as September 11th and rising security concerns. And many of us have dealt with the turbulence of the financial crisis, greater competition, and restructuring in the job market that in part fuel the gig and freelance economy.

The Type R mindset and skills couldn't be more appropriate to help us grapple with these realities and learn to thrive in the turmoil.

The Collective Type R Mindset

In 1963, when US president John F. Kennedy was assassinated in Dallas, the country mourned with Jacqueline Kennedy and struggled under the weight of the loss. Dallas was shrouded in silence, shamed by the tragic events and the fact that it was home to a loose-knit anti-Kennedy group made up of right-wing extremists. The city solemnly resigned itself to being labeled a "city of hate," as if to say "we have to accept that this is what we are."

For years, no monuments were erected, no ceremonies were held to mark the tragedy, and not a single street was renamed. The pent-up stress was revealed as suicide rates jumped to 20 percent in the year following Kennedy's assassination in comparison to the 1 percent national average.[4]

And yet just over fifty years later, when the city once again became the site of another tragedy, the people's response showed a significantly different mentality—one of growth, shared grieving, and collective effort to create change. On July 7, 2016, a sniper killed five police officers at a peaceful protest. Citizens had organized that day to draw attention to the number of deaths of African Americans they believed were killed by law enforcement officers because of their race. However, following the terrible events in 2016, the city and its residents appeared to be on a significantly different path as they grappled with racial tension and loss.

In the wake of the shootings, the words of the African American Dallas police chief, David Brown, offered condolence and a sense of calm while showing his own vulnerability. He spoke of turning hate into love over generations. And when he called on people to be a part of creating change and helping to resolve tensions in Dallas, within a two-week period he received an outpouring of more than four hundred applications to join the police force.

Barack Obama, the United States' first African American president, also sent a powerful message to Dallas and the world at a memorial service as he stood alongside former President George W. Bush, a member of the opposite political party. In his speech, Obama emphasized his belief in the city's and the nation's ability to collectively shift their view of the events, reframing to transform tragedy into strength. "We know that suffering produces perseverance; perseverance, character; and character, hope," Obama told the crowd. "We do not persevere alone. Our character is not found in isolation. I believe our sorrow can make us a better country. I believe our righteous anger can be transformed into more justice and more peace," he concluded.[5]

Rather than feeling that Dallas was a place of shame, the collective mindset had shifted. This was reflected in the way that the city and its residents acknowledged the tragic events and embarked on the process of healing, knowing that challenges remain and years of work lie ahead.

"In '63, we were having discussions on, 'Are we really a people that hate?' Now, we're probably setting the tone for how we should discuss race in America, policing in America," said Carol Reed, a long-time local political strategist. Other residents like Miguel Solis, thirty, a member of the Dallas School Board, pointed out that the city has been through several difficult periods. "At every one of those miserable times we could have stopped and let the misery define us, but we don't. We persevere," he said.

The question that arises in the face of challenges like those in Dallas is, Do we focus on our limitations and collectively catastrophize in the face of challenge, or do we focus on the cracks where the light seeps in and invest in a belief that we are able to grow?

To answer this question and get at the essence of how we cultivate positive, collective Type R mindsets, we have to take into account that for hundreds of years groups of all sizes, races, and denominations have grappled with cohesion and the extent to which we cultivate collective belief systems or ways of viewing the world and our place in it. In the eighteenth century, the

French sociologist Émile Durkheim introduced the idea of collective consciousness—an early way of describing our shared beliefs, ideas, and moral attitudes that operate as a unifying force in a society.[6] Durkheim discovered that we are a product of our environment. And to be able to shift collective mindsets, we have to understand the group's starting point and the origins of its existing beliefs.

Think of the common expressions that give us a window into the collective attitude of whole nations or cultures, particularly as they relate to adversity and challenge. There is the British expression, to have a "stiff upper lip," urging more than one generation to practice restraint and not to show their emotions when they're upset. Then there's the American adage, "When life gives you lemons, make lemonade," cheerily encouraging people to have a "can-do" attitude and make the best with what they're given.

Sayings such as these provide some insight into how we convey a mindset and frame adversity from generation to generation, and in so doing create a strong sense of identity. This is especially true when bits of wisdom like this are passed down to us by loved ones or people we respect.

Perhaps what has changed today, to some extent, is the way in which we communicate mindsets. Social structures have become more complex, and technology facilitates rapid-fire and wide-reaching information sharing across cultures and nations.

Someone like Jonathan Blake can pinpoint specific factors that influenced his outlook and ability to reframe his challenging circumstances—his family upbringing, a positive disposition, and being presented with a situation in which he had "nothing to lose." But group mindsets have multiple layers and influencing factors that we must acknowledge in the process of cultivating a collective Type R mindset and working to reframe existing beliefs.

More often than not we don't even recognize our shared views until they're challenged or are put in contrast with others. Group attitudes are particularly powerful, given that other people and groups play a large role in our search for confirmation and validation of our own beliefs.

As social beings, we often crave a sense of belonging and are influenced by others' viewpoints and emotions. As a result, whether we adopt a Type R mindset or opt for less productive perspectives is influenced in part by the company that we keep and the mindsets of the groups we are a part of.

Sociologist Thomas Scheff at the University of California, Santa Barbara, further sheds light on what may encourage or inhibit a shift to a collective Type R mindset. His research suggests that the anticipation of being rewarded or punished for falling in line with a group is so strong that we forecast the response subconsciously. As a result, we defer to others in invisible ways that guarantee alignment of thoughts, feelings, and actions among individuals and groups, or even nations.

Perhaps most impactful is Scheff's conclusion that this chain reaction of what he calls the emotion-deference system between and within groups can last longer than a lifetime, passing from generation to generation.[7] This suggests that mindsets themselves and Type R skills specifically can be handed down through the years and that the way we frame adversity and challenge could influence others decades into the future.

In a similar way to individuals, groups—from circles of friends to families, organizations, and businesses—can employ the Type R characteristics and skills as a path to transformation. Groups can also prove to be important sources of support in reinforcing positive mindsets and in creating an important sense of belonging that allows many to thrive.

Take, for instance, the research that Carol Dweck and her colleagues undertook on how negative assumptions about women's math skills has affected young women. In one study, researchers tracked female math students in college calculus courses in northeastern American universities. They wanted to know how mindset protected the students from or exposed them to the limiting perspectives of others and the adverse experiences of facing negative stereotyping.

After surveying the young women and separating them into two groups, those with fixed mindsets and those with more robust mindsets, the researchers interviewed the women at various points in the course and asked questions about what they thought of math and if they felt like they belonged in the mathematics community.

The women with a fixed and less robust mindset and those with less social support seemed to become increasingly alienated. They were particularly affected by the negative views of one professor, who framed female knowledge of the course material as a "good guess" when students correctly answered a question in class. Over the semester, the students seemed to allow the negative views of others to define them and showed an eroding sense of belonging in the math course. It's not surprising that this was accompanied by a decrease in final grades in the course and reduced intentions of female students to study math in the future.[8]

In comparison, the women with a more resilient and growth-oriented mindset were disturbed by the stereotypes, but they reframed and separated the poor behavior of professors and others from their own abilities and continued to thrive. They maintained a sense of belonging even when they faced prejudice and setbacks that were devastating for others.

These female students were also members of groups that appeared to strengthen their positive beliefs. One of the students described the same professor's bias against women's input in class and the countering effect of the group by saying, "It was absurd and reflected poorly on the instructor. . . . [But] it was also all right because we were working in groups and we were able to give and receive support among us students. . . . We discussed our interesting ideas among ourselves."[9] Clearly, the groups supported the young women's own positive and resilient framing along with their continued learning and growth. The group mindset and the social support countered the limiting effects of this professor's views and those of the wider academic environment and community.

In complementary and parallel ways, groups with a Type R outlook can reframe the prejudices, impediments, challenges, and stresses they face and incorporate them into their own process of growth and problem solving. They also often find that these challenges serve to create greater cohesion, support, and understanding among themselves.

We must acknowledge that it's unlikely that everyone in a group will have the same starting point with respect to the Type R mindset and its supporting characteristics and behaviors or will even feel the same way about embracing change. That said, a shift toward Type R can be as simple as having one person introduce a new, compelling frame for addressing adversity that others—whether they're leaders, followers, agnostics, or supporters of the shared will of the group—can build on. As we discuss in Chapter 5, the ripple effect and impact of a single person are significant.

Returning to Ellen Langer's Counterclockwise study, one older participant named Fred, who had a particularly positive and engaged outlook, inspired the others in the study, helping them immerse themselves in the belief that they were young and capable again. "Fred was a bit different and goaded some of the others into doing more than they were used to doing," wrote Langer. "To their surprise everything fell into place. Instead of presuming that they 'couldn't' do something they got with the program and were successful."

That isn't to say that change takes place immediately. But a Type R individual, leader, colleague, or family member can serve as an important catalyst for altering how we collectively frame the challenges we face and the ways we view the world around us.

The Power of Hope

One of the most powerful elements in our ability to grow and change is having hope. But that requires that we sit with uncertainty. "Hope locates itself in the premises that we don't know what will happen and that in the spaciousness of uncertainty is room to act," according to Rebecca Solnit, a Guggenheim fellow and widely acclaimed author who writes about history and social change, among other topics. "When you recognize uncertainty, you recognize that you may be able to influence the outcomes—you alone or you in concert with a few dozen or several million others."[10]

While we might tend to grasp for the certainty of optimism, with its reassurance of a positive outcome, or pessimism, with its certainty of a negative conclusion, hope requires that we adopt a positive framing while not drawing conclusions in ways that will stunt our growth and the possibilities to come.

It was hope and the ability to give himself permission to see what came next and engage in life that got Jonathan Blake through some of his toughest times in the early days of living with HIV. It is hope that is knitting together communities in Dallas as people there continue to grieve while growing and looking for solutions to today's challenges. But people like Jonathan and communities like Dallas go beyond hope to the fundamentals of Type R that are rooted in the belief that something positive can emerge from hardship.

Regardless of our current beliefs, it's always possible to cultivate a Type R mindset that will support us in more effectively coping with adversity. Thriving in the face of challenges is a matter of attitude. It's not the result of good luck or superior genetics but of learning how to forge meaning from whatever happens to us.

By rethinking how we perceive adversity, stress, and disruptive change, we can alter their effect on our physical health, well-being, life satisfaction, and ability to marshal the intellectual, emotional, and physical resources needed for our changing world. In other words, when we alter our mindset, we change the outlook for the future and what's possible.

Type Rs see challenge as a door to continual learning. And like the older adults turned young again in Langer's studies, Type Rs transform themselves through the power of mindset and the way it guides their beliefs, behaviors, and relationships.

Psychologist C. R. Snyder researched hope and found it to be a result of struggle—a collection of learned behaviors garnered from adversity. Working with hundreds of different study groups, he concluded that hope is a pathway to attain our goals for the future and a belief in our own abilities, a linking of our present to an imagined future.[11]

To survive and thrive in this rapidly changing world, what we need, above all else, are the skills to embrace uncertainty as a fact of life, knowing that we have the resources to meet the challenges we will inevitably face. In this respect, the Type R mindset is hopeful: the six characteristics that support it provide a path forward to our goals, whether personal, professional, or global. But the largest, overarching goal is to better equip ourselves to face our changing, stressful, and at times traumatic world and circumstances.

CHAPTER 4

Harnessing the Storm: The Type R Characteristics

Adversity is like a strong wind. It tears away from us all but the things that cannot be torn, so that we see ourselves as we really are.

Arthur Golden

MANY OF US remember the opening of the film *Mary Poppins*: a line of sullen nannies dressed in black gather outside the London home of the Banks family to interview for a job taking care of their children. Suddenly, a storm arrives. The nannies' umbrellas turn inside out and crumple, becoming completely useless. The nannies clutch fences and lampposts as the force of the wind rips off their hats and then whisks them away.

But there's one woman who stands out from the rest—her umbrella isn't like the others'; it not only endures but also carries her to her destination. Against a dark sky, Mary Poppins rides in gracefully, her umbrella harnessing the storm as it delivers her to the Banks' front door, perfectly composed while the wind whips around her.

Together, the Type R characteristics are a bit like Mary Poppins's umbrella. They may shade us from the heat of life's changes and challenges and the drenching rain of storm clouds. But, more than a shelter under which to retreat during life's storms, they are an umbrella that takes us on a journey and delivers us to a new place rife with opportunity.

Amid the turbulence of chaos and change, we can't expect that we'll simply sail in, arriving at our destination without a single hair out of place, perfectly composed, and unscathed by the experience. Luckily, that's not the intention, expectation, or even the goal—the journey and the transformation that it enables matter most.

The unique demands of today's complex and ever-changing world require a set of tools specifically suited for the age in which we live. We need to prepare ourselves for the distinctive challenges we will face and apply our skills in appropriate and effective ways. So, let's explore the six characteristics that individuals and groups can employ to cultivate the Type R mindset, skills, and behaviors.

The Six Characteristics

Through our research and our years of experience with everyone from friends, coworkers, and family members to corporate and world leaders, we've found six characteristics and skills that allow for Transformative Resilience.

Like the first parasols, which were made up of six panels and a framework of six supports, Type R is held up by various spokes, or, in this case, characteristics. Though it can continue to function without one or even two of them, it is strongest and most effective when all of them work together. The fundamental equation is as follows:

Adaptability
Healthy relationship to control
Continual learning
Sense of purpose
Leveraging support
Active engagement

These qualities reinforce and interact with one another in multiple ways as well as having merit on their own. And they apply not only to individuals but also to leaders, organizations, and families and can be developed and strengthened over time.

If we have the proper framing and the understanding that most of us will experience immense change and a major stressful life event at some point, then we can live not in fear but with anticipation. We can take steps to be prepared to meet challenges with the intention of finding the transformative goals within them.

The Type R Characteristics

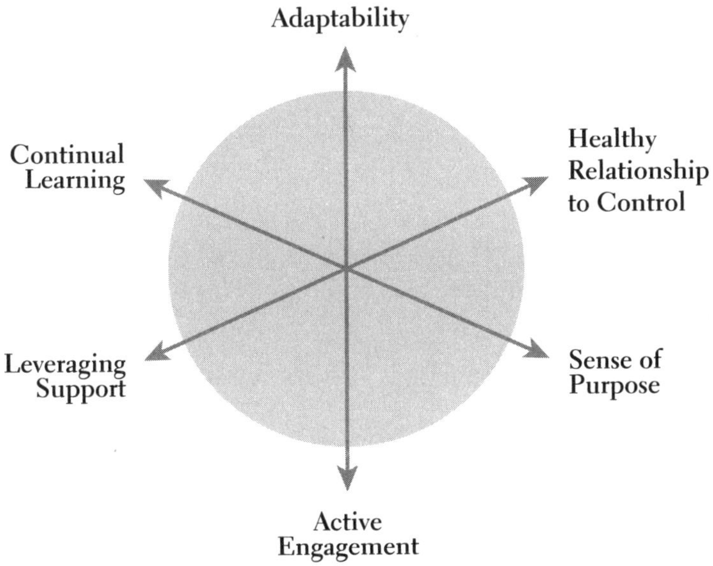

If we can imagine things as they never were and participate in the experimentation and innovation necessary to create new solutions, if we can reassert our purpose and integrity as we live through adversity, we can turn hardship and change to our advantage for a hopeful future. The silver lining is that with the Type R mindset and skills we can use challenging experiences to set us on a path to grow and thrive.

Take, for example, Akira Thompson. At the age of nineteen, Akira joined the US Army. He hoped his service would give him the funds to eventually return to his studies, which he had temporarily put aside, and his dream of using media and games to examine culture in ways that are both entertaining and enlightening.

In 2003 Akira was sent to Iraq, where he was assigned to transport soldiers and equipment. His unit experienced several mortar attacks on the base where he was stationed. And he regularly drove through dangerous terrain, where dissidents drove cars up alongside US Army convoys and detonated bombs. One of his most devastating memories was of the day he misjudged the force of his five-ton truck as he tried to edge a blue Cadillac over to the shoulder of the road to keep the convoy safe.

Instead, he ran over the car only later to learn it contained an entire family, including a grandmother and a baby. Luckily, they were unscathed, but this experience and others like it, along with the effects of the United States' deteriorating relationship with the Iraqi people, made him grapple with his humanity. Later he came face to face with the grandmother. "Never before had I seen someone look at me with such hate," he says when we speak to him, recalling the interaction. "I deserved it. I could have really hurt them."[1]

When Akira returned from his deployment in the spring of 2004, he re-enrolled in college and began to study animation. "I wanted to use my talents and passion for media to do something that would make a positive change that could hopefully now outweigh the negativity that I had also played a part in spreading."

But life was fraught with difficulty. After graduating, he found a promising media job, but it lasted only a few months because of the collapse of the US economy. And so Akira found himself underemployed, working in a minimum-wage job at a teashop in Chicago. Often the only way that he could afford to eat was to wait for the leftovers thrown out at the café each night.

It was a particularly depressing time for Akira. Aside from his financial concerns, because he couldn't find work he felt that he had failed at his goal of discovering a way to use media to effect positive change. "I reached the darkest point where I was contemplating ending everything and am really grateful that I didn't," he explains.

But reaching such a low also triggered a realization that he had to make a change. Around that time, a friend of his left for Los Angeles to start a new job, so Akira also decided to make the move out West in search of opportunity and a new life.

Not long after arriving in California, Akira found temporary work testing video games. He had a number of seasonal jobs, but he often felt lonely living in a new place, and he continued to struggle emotionally as well as financially. However, he was persistent, and eventually secured a job in the Research and Development Department of Walt Disney's Imagineering.

At the time, Akira expected that he'd find a stable job and then he'd work other things out. But the opposite proved to be true. "Once I was able to sort my [emotional] stuff out then other positive things came along. After I was able to establish that, then I was able to feel a sense of normalcy," he says, reflecting on the following years as he attended to his psychological struggles and built his career and personal life.

He thrived in his job, and in 2011 he found himself on the Forbes list of "30 Under 30 in Entertainment" alongside people like actresses Lena Dunham and Jennifer Lawrence. But he didn't stop there. Although Disney provided a stable base for him, after a while he knew it was time to create something of his own.

Finally, in 2012, he founded an independent company called RainBros, which designs games that help its players build empathy and understand issues like racism and economic inequality by immersing them in the experience of other people. It provided the social outlet that he sought all along. He also enrolled in a master's degree program in games and playable media at the University of California at Santa Cruz's Computer Science Department to further his skills and the development of his company.

Akira's experiences in the army and his later struggles to find work and financial stability could have defeated him. Instead, they were the basis for who he has become. Today he is married and is living in Japan, where his company is working with Universal Studios on a number of projects designing immersive-experience games.

People like Akira remind us that many of us struggle in our own ways, whether in our careers, in our personal lives, or in finding our place in the world—and often in all three. The difference is what we do with these struggles. Akira demonstrates many of the Type R characteristics and skills. And, yet, like Akira, as Type Rs we don't always use all of these skills all the time and don't always have all of them developed in equal measure, but we continue to learn, grow, and strengthen these abilities.

Adaptability

More than 150 years ago, in his description of natural selection, Charles Darwin wrote, "It is not the strongest of the species that survive, nor the most intelligent, but the one most responsive to change."

As we've seen with Akira, to successfully cope with the changing circumstances of our lives we have to strike a delicate balance—a negotiation between knowing when to hold firm and when to accept the changing world around us and alter our outlook, goals, and plans.

"Adaptability was one of the only things that most [helped]. Grit is important, but if you're unable to shift gears when 'grit' isn't working, you don't get anywhere," says Akira. "Where there was a closed door I was able to shift my focus and start looking at what doors could be opened," he says, explaining that it was still a lengthy process of adaptation.

But Akira's process of evolving hasn't just been about pivoting and taking advantage of geographical or career opportunities. He has also been gradually adapting his beliefs to better fit who he has become through the years. In nature, adaptability is what permitted organisms from as early as 3.5 billion years ago not only to survive but also to thrive in highly changeable and very difficult circumstances.

In a study researchers in the Animal Physiology Department of the University of Groningen in the Netherlands conducted, mice that had been trained for rote memorization and that therefore relied on routine, rigid behavior, and fixed expectations of their environment to guide them to the end of a labyrinth performed poorly when the course of the maze was changed. On the other hand, mice that took cues from their actual environment and adapted cognitively and behaviorally to their changing circumstances performed significantly better.[2]

Of equal importance for people is psychological flexibility, or the ability to use the right emotional resources at the right times in order to adapt. According to Todd Kashdan, a psychology professor at the George Mason University in Virginia, and Jonathan Rottenberg, a professor at the University of South Florida, psychological flexibility spans a wide range of human abilities, including recognizing and adapting to various demands; shifting our mindsets when current strategies compromise our ability to function;

balancing competing desires and needs; and being aware, open, and committed to behaviors that are in line with our deeply held values. Essentially, psychological flexibility means that people have to adapt to their surroundings on an ongoing basis.[3]

Akira realized that he couldn't solve all of his problems by changing locations or focusing on career goals—he had to get to the heart of the emotional challenges he faced. He realized that he needed to make an internal shift and begin working on himself to try to solve some of those issues. It wasn't until then that he was able to move beyond the pain and emotional difficulty that had been holding him back. A large part of that change was discovering what resonated with him versus what he had been taught when he was growing up. He had to think about how these overlapped as well as how they differed.

While individuals like Akira grapple with these issues, large numbers of organizations and companies are also realizing that they have to be more nimble and adaptable in order to thrive. To keep afloat, some organizations have had to dramatically reinvent themselves, from breaking into entirely new markets to trading brick-and-mortar outlets for an online presence.

For instance, Disney has continually redefined its business model, positioning itself as a provider of entertainment, not merely a maker of cartoons, its original business. This has allowed the company to continually reinvent itself and secure every new opportunity that occurs in its sector.

Along with the acknowledgment that unpredictability is now permanent comes the recognition that chaos is part of the new world order. As much as adaptability is essential in times of uncertainty, we instinctively become more cautious; we look to the past, to times that seemed simpler, and we have the urge to try to repeat them. This approach can make us rigid and resist change.

Yet twenty-first-century success requires us to develop adaptability, meaning we should welcome—or even invite—more opportunities to cultivate this essential quality, however unsettling it may be. Adaptability must become a building block for contemporary life. While some people may be shaken by sudden change, Type Rs adapt and prosper. However, that often means taking a closer look at what we can and cannot control.

Healthy Relationship to Control

"All the art of living lies in a fine mingling of letting go and holding on," according to the British physician Havelock Ellis, who was, among other things, a writer and public intellectual best known for introducing the notion of narcissism in the early 1900s. This is our challenge in discovering a healthy relationship to control: we must strike just the right balance between recognizing when to exert control, to persevere, and when to let go.

In the 1960s American psychologist Julian Rotter investigated how people's behaviors and attitudes affected the outcomes of their lives. He found that some people believe they're essentially in control of the good and bad things they experience. These people have what he called an internal locus of control. At the same time, there are other people who believe that things over which they have no control happen to them, pointing to an external locus. He concluded that these worldviews aren't absolute and that many people have both.[4]

We must take into account socioeconomic factors that prevent some of us from exerting agency or control over some fundamental circumstances in our lives and the decisions we make about basic needs. That said, where we believe the locus of control resides in our lives says a lot about how much agency we believe we have and how developed our sense of our own capabilities is. As the world around us changes, so too does our understanding of how to be successful and live well.

Believing that we control the outcomes of our lives and our successes isn't only empowering but also a starting point for creating Transformative Resilience. Yet, focusing too intensely on an internal locus of control and our ability to control has significant downsides.

Stress is less likely to be damaging if people feel they have some control over the circumstance.[5] But, often, that may extend only as far as our ability to choose how we frame a situation and how we respond to it. If we're inclined to have an optimistic outlook and the self-confidence that we can survive a difficult period, we're more likely to have a positive response than if we perceive stress as disastrous.

Our conversations with researchers like Mark Seery, whose studies on adversity we discussed in Chapter 2, reconfirm that having a sense of control can level the playing field in terms of who is able to be resilient in the face of stress and challenge.

In a recent study he and his colleagues conducted, participants underwent a pain experiment. This built upon the earlier research that demonstrated the toughening factor of having some exposure to adversity and investigated the role that control plays. Per Seery's earlier work, those with low exposure as well as those with high exposure to adversity demonstrated less-resilient responses to stress or physical pain. And those with medium levels of exposure to adversity had more-resilient responses. Once that was established, half of the participants were asked to choose an envelope before the next part of the study began. They were led to believe the contents of the envelope dictated the pain treatment they would receive. Meanwhile, the other participants simply received the pain treatment.[6]

The researchers found that people with both low and high levels of exposure to adversity responded significantly better when given an opportunity to choose an envelope and feel that they had somehow participated in deciding the treatment they would receive. Being given the perception of having control led these participants to report lower levels of pain and fewer feelings of overwhelm.

Seery concludes that giving these people a sense of control allows them to have a response on par with those who have been "toughened" by some exposure to adversity. "I wouldn't argue that we can control everything around us, but finding slivers of control when slivers are available can help people to successfully cope," he says.

The control that people actually have or perceive that they have is an important motivator of either helpless or resilient behavior. If we believe that nothing we do matters, we fall victim to a sense that we are powerless and become passive and limited in our coping abilities. On the other hand, when we believe that we can influence events and outcomes to some extent, we make active attempts to overcome adversity and create change.[7]

But there are limits to how healthy or helpful being in control can be. If we believe that we and we alone are responsible for what happens to us or we have an extreme internal locus of control, we can take on too much responsibility for ourselves and the world around us. This tendency can be a huge source of stress and difficulty because it doesn't sufficiently take into account external factors, and it can cause us to be overly rigid.

Wendy R. Anderson is a woman used to being in control in every sense of the word. In just a few years, she went from being a graduate student to becoming one of the most senior national security advisers in the US government. In the process Wendy was significantly influenced by the culture of the Department of Defense, which has a top-down management structure and an ethos of decisiveness even when things don't go to plan. It is also an environment dominated by men, where women work harder to be seen as competent authorities. But that authority, Wendy has come to understand, has its downsides, which made her question her habits once she was offered a leadership job in a different government department.

"Control of staff, control of an agency—I never knew how to let go of that [impulse]. I don't know very well how to be relaxed in a situation like that," Wendy explains. "It's the difference between the fist and the open palm."[8]

A lot of Wendy's behavior and what she had learned about leadership were ineffective in her new work environment. "I behaved in a way that was tight and alienated my colleagues, especially subordinates, rather than being open, solicitous, and inclusive. I felt I had no real control. Instead of inviting people into my uncertainty about this new agency and asking for help, I hunkered down and inevitably ended up shutting down," she says. Moving forward, Wendy has tried to be curious about her behavior rather than criticizing herself, which had become her tendency over a number of years. She is instead reflecting, learning new skills, and testing them out as she begins to work with teams in different ways (as we will hear more about in the next chapter).

People spend a considerable amount of precious time trying to control the uncontrollable or fearing a loss of control and overexerting themselves in attempts to gain or maintain a sense of power. Fear of the unknown is natural in the face of change and challenge. But, as Type Rs, we trust that no matter what happens, we possess the inner resources to cope. We're buoyed by confidence that we can influence some of the basic elements of our lives and shoulder any consequences that are beyond our control. As a result, we can let go. We don't need to micromanage and command the world in an attempt to protect ourselves. We are confident we can handle anything and can loosen our grip and open ourselves to all sorts of possibilities that aren't there when we are attached to only one right way.

As Type Rs, we've learned to assess what's within our sphere of influence and what's not. We realize that strength isn't always determined by triumph over the outside world but sometimes by changing our inner world. As a result, we can respond appropriately, investing energy in areas where we have influence, acknowledging and shifting focus away from areas where we don't, and redirecting our energy into cultivating Transformative Resilience.

To have a healthier relationship with control, we must embrace what is rather than wishing for what's not. When we accept life on its own terms, we discover whatever positive experiences and opportunities may be possible in a given situation. Having greater perspective on what we control and what we don't creates a tremendous sense of relief. But, most importantly, it allows us to learn from the circumstances life presents us with.

Continual Learning

We each carry around an internal map of the world—a map of our professional and personal landscape and of our social, emotional, economic, or political terrain. In the same way that we update maps to reflect a changing world, we have to update our understanding of ourselves, the situations we encounter, our surroundings, and the world we live in. If change or adversity transforms our personal or professional landscape, figuratively or literally, we have to relearn this territory—assess opportunities, risks, allies, available resources, and tools needed to not only survive but also prosper.

Futurist and author Alvin Toffler once said that the illiterate of the twenty-first century won't be those who can't read and write but those who can't learn, unlearn, and relearn. How right he was—and still is!

Luckily, our brains are hardwired to learn from stress as well as from our environment. Stanford University researchers demonstrated that after a stressful event our brains secrete DHEA, a neurosteroid that helps the brain grow, recover, and gain new knowledge from experience.[9]

That's not to say that all stresses are the same, as we previously mentioned. But on a basic level we are meant to extract new information from the threats, challenges, and stresses we experience so that we can plan ahead and keep them from recurring. We prepare for new challenges and can better understand the environment as it evolves. Fortunately, we don't have to be under stress to learn, and learning is cumulative, accruing and building on previous layers of experience.

For the first decade or two of our lives, learning is our primary "job." A lot of our time is spent in school gaining knowledge. In the Eastern European Jewish tradition, it was thought that the act of learning itself was so valuable that it should be associated with sweetness. For this reason, children were given cookies in the shapes of each letter of the alphabet topped with a dollop of honey.

However, once we graduate, many of us feel like the education chapter is over and it is now time to enter the "real" world. Yet this attitude closes us to a lifetime of lessons garnered through experience, observation, experimentation, and trials and tribulations.

Individuals and groups that remain curious tend to gravitate to new skills, new experiences, and new networks. This is particularly important given that research from the University of California, Davis, suggests that when our curiosity is piqued, changes in the brain ready us to acquire knowledge not only about the subject at hand but also about related information. "Curiosity may put the brain in a state that allows it to attain and retain any kind of information, like a vortex that sucks in what you are motivated to learn, and also everything around it," said Dr. Matthias Gruber, lead author of the study.[10]

In other words, curious brains are dynamic brains, and dynamic brains become smart brains. Curiosity is also connected with high performance. Evidence increasingly suggests a relationship between curiosity and knowledge. The more we learn, the more we desire to learn. To be successful, we *must* be curious. This is as true for individuals as it is for teams of people in organizations.

To use adversity to our advantage, we have to become keen observers of our inner world through self-awareness and self-assessment. The great thinkers of history offer us guidance. Diogenes implored, "Know thyself"; Shakespeare said, "To thine own self be true"; Plato cautioned, "The unexamined life is not worth living." The more we know about what makes us tick, what we're good at, where our vulnerabilities lie, and what resources we have, the easier it is for us to adapt when things change.

Learning provides us with deeper meaning and greater internal resources to bring to the stress and adversity we encounter. Frequently, learning leads to a sense of purpose or hope, which places immediate difficulties into a wider perspective and shifts people's focus away from daily stress.[11] Curiosity and continual learning are essential for building TR and improving our ability to deal with disruptive change, whether individually or collectively, and to find meaning in it.

Type Rs remain curious throughout life and seek opportunities to broaden their knowledge and skills, even when there's not always an obvious need for doing so. They are interested in both their internal experience and the outer world. This curiosity is vital to adaptability and intellectual growth, and it motivates ongoing learning and forward motion.

Sense of Purpose

Amid the quakes and tremors of the times we live in, it's easy to lose our footing and to get disoriented, particularly when the ground beneath us shakes with any degree of magnitude. We need a new compass, not one that we hold in our hand but a truer, internal compass—a sense of purpose, something that gives our lives and our actions an underlying cause or significance.

In a study published in the *Journal of Positive Psychology,* researchers asked nearly four hundred Americans between the ages of eighteen and seventy-eight years whether they thought their lives were meaningful and/or happy. The study found that, although experiencing negative events decreased participants' level of happiness, it increased the amount of meaning they had in their lives. An earlier study corroborates these results, finding that people who have meaning in their lives through a clearly defined sense of purpose rate their life satisfaction higher than those who do not have a clearly defined purpose. This holds even when people struggled and were feeling down.[12]

Additionally, researchers have found that a sense of purpose creates physical as well as life span benefits. For instance, having a high sense of purpose in life may lower risk for heart disease and stroke. Developing and improving a sense of purpose can protect heart health and even potentially save our lives. According to research at Mount Sinai Medical Center, purpose was associated with a 23 percent reduction in death from all causes and a 19 percent reduced risk of heart attack and stroke.[13]

Type R individuals, leaders, organizations, and families have a strong sense of purpose and meaning that anchors and guides them. Having meaning in our lives helps us face difficulties and overcome hardship. A sense of purpose gives us a reason to aim for something and is especially important when we're confronted with adversity.

Purpose also links us to the experiences of others and something larger than ourselves. It stretches us beyond our limited perspective and isolation of our challenges, stress, or adversity and urges us to channel our energy in focused and productive ways.

As mentioned earlier, for people like Akira, adaptability plays a large role in eventual transformation, but so too does a sense of purpose. Throughout Akira's struggles, a common thread provided continuity, superseded his challenges, and gave him both hope and drive as he worked toward using his media and game development skills to immerse people in others' experiences and help them build empathy.

When Akira started a job in Hollywood in a new "showy" environment and found himself straying from his goals, he was able to find his way back, using his strong sense of purpose and increasingly solidifying beliefs to guide him.

Akira's growing internal strength and sense of purpose also built his confidence and allowed him to make important contributions to the groups and organizations that he worked with. "I was able to hold my head high and be self-assured about who I was and what I was aiming to do. It allowed me to put time into things that I cared about deeply without me needing to [be] rewarded," he explains. Once some of his internal challenges were resolved, external opportunities fell into place.

A sense of purpose also anchors groups of people and provides tools for overcoming challenges. Take, for instance, Warby Parker, one of today's most successful start-ups. The company set out to make good, affordable eyewear and to contribute to positive social outcomes by donating a pair of eyeglasses to someone in need for every pair sold.[14] This sense of purpose has repeatedly steadied the company in the challenging and turbulent world of entrepreneurship as well as helped it deal with difficulties, such as the fallout from misjudged market responses and the tangled process of delivering glasses to developing countries.

People and organizations with a strong sense of purpose use their values as their compass. These values keep them on course regardless of the chaos, confusion, or challenges they face. Type Rs maintain a vision of what truly matters, what their lives and their work are about, and what they want it to be. A sense of purpose provides a buffer against obstacles; a person or group with a strong sense of purpose can more easily remain engaged and satisfied with life or work even while experiencing challenges.

No one better reminds us of the importance of finding purpose and meaning, even in the face of the most difficult situations, than Viktor Frankl. In the 1930s, with the Nazi horror looming, Frankl, a well-known Jewish neurologist and psychiatrist, made the decision to stay with his parents in Vienna despite the fact that he had the opportunity to leave.

In September 1942, Frankl was arrested, along with his pregnant wife and parents, and was deported to a concentration camp. Three years later, when his camp was liberated, his family, including his pregnant wife, had died—but he had survived.

He determined that what separated those who had lived from those who had died in the camp was purpose: the people who found a reason to live even in those most unbearable conditions were far more resilient to anguish than those who did not. "Those who have a 'why' to live, can bear with almost any 'how.'"[15]

Frankl's experience may reflect what researchers have found in subsequent years that not only does a sense of purpose anchor us emotionally but also it provides us with physical strength, greater life satisfaction, and reduced stress. When difficult situations arise, it's all too human to ask, Why did this have to happen to me? To my family? To my organization? To my community? Being able to make sense of stressful life events, challenges, and trauma, to find meaning in what has happened, and to contextualize the events within our understanding of a greater sense of purpose is essential for transforming distress into something more useful.

Making sense of what has taken place, drawing meaning from it, and understanding how that serves or supports our sense of purpose can act as a beacon that provides direction in our day-to-day lives. What matters to those facing adversity and change is a sense of understanding that life does indeed make sense, despite chaos, stress, worry, or despair. Type Rs also hold on to a sense of hope that gives meaning and order to challenge and helps us recognize a clear narrative that connects the future to the past and the present. It's therefore no surprise that a sense of purpose as well as hope play significant roles in TR, helping us re-evaluate and adjust our priorities and the trajectories of our lives and work.

In troubled times, when we are stripped of what we hold dear we have an opportunity to get in touch with what truly matters. When everything we struggle to hold on to falls apart, we're left in the present moment to re-evaluate our values and sense of purpose and, if need be, to adjust our priorities, direction, and the trajectory of our lives. This often means calling on those around us.

Leveraging Support

In the fall of 2008, after the stock market crashed, Jill Warren, deputy director of one of the world's largest and most recognized not-for-profits, found herself making cuts, laying people off, and restructuring the organization. This exhausted her and forced her to shift her focus away from the issues she most cared about, which opened the door for a head hunter to approach her about leading a small international health organization.

Although it wasn't apparent at the time, the role would become what's called a "glass cliff" scenario, where women and people of color find themselves in leadership positions during periods of crisis when the chance of failure is high. And still, over the next few years, Jill was able to navigate an extremely challenging situation in large part by leveraging the support of experts, colleagues, friends, and family.

She did a significant amount of due diligence, talking to the board and the finance department and looking over the budget. When everything checked out, she accepted the job and dove in. "There was a wonderful honeymoon. I loved the staff. I loved the work," explains Jill when we speak with her.[16]

But she soon discovered that some well-intentioned albeit "creative" accounting was masking the organization's financial shortfall. She confronted the accountant and stemmed the problem at its root, but significant issues had been hidden for some time. To devise financial solutions, she first turned to a team of experts from New York University to help her create an aggressive fund-raising plan. However, when it became obvious that the organization was in a dire financial situation that required more immediate action, Jill relied on the support of others.

"I remember crying every night for two weeks when I was having these calls with the [board]," Jill says, recalling the immense stress she was under and her reluctance to reveal her level of distress to her staff while proposing different options.

Peter, an organizational management expert whom Jill had worked with in her previous job, met with her regularly and acted as a sounding board. He often did so as a friend when she didn't have funding to pay him. That, along with support of her family, helped Jill get the organization through the challenging times and helped her grapple with her feelings of failure as she moved on to the next stages of her career. These conversations were freeing and clarifying. Jill returned to the board and convinced it to implement the emergency financial plans that she had put forward, which it had been resisting. At the same time, Jill decided that she should resign, given that her expertise in advocacy was not what was most needed in this time of transition.

"It was a pretty dark time for me.... Lots of nonprofits had closed. My field was smaller. It felt like I was very difficult to place," she says. "It was so scary thinking, 'Maybe I'll never have another job. Maybe my career is over.'"

While Jill went through a lengthy period of unemployment, she was buoyed by the encouragement of her husband of more than twenty years, who had always been an important base of support. She ultimately secured a management position at a large intergovernmental organization.

"I frequently had moments with Peter where he would capture something and make me reflect on it and then I would see it in a different way and I would be able to act quite differently," Jill recalls. "It really helped me to have breakthroughs." Peter's support, for instance, helped Jill understand her core values and the fact that her commitment to seeing a group or a cause that she cares about do well has also led her to make sacrifices that at times are at great expense to her personally.

The truth is that we get by with a little help from our friends, to paraphrase the Beatles. In fact, our social and professional networks do far more than simply help us "get by." They significantly contribute to our physical, mental, and emotional well-being. The perspectives of trusted people help us think outside the limitations of our own outlook, knowledge, or resources. They not only provide a different outlook on the situation but also sometimes more importantly help us see ourselves in a new way. Leveraging support helps buffer us from the negative effects of stress and enables us to flourish either because of or in spite of our circumstances.[17]

One of the biggest obstacles to growing from adversity is the sense of being alone. Many of us feel ashamed when we're suffering and retreat into isolation and avoidance. We don't want to show our vulnerability or weakness.

However, when we feel isolated it's more difficult to have the perspective we need to see the potential opportunity in our hardship. Isolation can also interfere with our ability to reach out to others, especially at a time when so many of those around us project a trouble-free life or picture-perfect business on social media. This may be especially true for women, people of color, LGBT people, and younger people, who often feel that they have to prove themselves, particularly in the workplace, and as a result don't ask for help to mobilize the support they need. Although we may assume that we're alone in our struggles, the reality is that nothing is more universal than the experience of stressful life events.

Our challenge is to remember this when we're struggling, even if our impulse is to withdraw and avoid connection. This is the exact time when we need to reach out to our network and ask for their understanding and support. Far from signaling weakness, connection and interdependence with others are essential building blocks of TR.

Support from our friends, families, colleagues, and communities has very real physical benefits as well. In one of the most famous experiments on health and social life, Sheldon Cohen at Carnegie Mellon University exposed hundreds of healthy volunteers to the common cold virus, then quarantined them for several days.[18] Cohen showed that the study participants with more social connections and with more diverse social networks—that is, with friends from a variety of social contexts, such as work, sports teams, and church—were less likely to develop a cold than the more socially isolated study participants.

Brain imaging also reveals the neurological differences between people who are alone and people who have support in times of stress: when placed under strain in a laboratory setting, the brain's stress response, which is demonstrated by activity in the anterior cingulate cortex region, is reduced when people have a close friend or relative with them.[19]

The idea of people enduring life's challenges on their own is misguided. Type Rs have a strong appreciation for social support and count family, friends, and colleagues among their most valuable resources. Type R individuals also have a strong sense of self. They can share vulnerability, doubts, and struggles with their intimate circle and readily ask for help and support. And they often seek out support from a range of professionals—whether psychologists, emergency services providers, or technical and business advisers—to get the resources they need that their social circles may not provide.

Type Rs instinctually know the benefits of networks and leverage support as part of their strategy for weathering change and adversity and building Transformative Resilience. They also understand that different people offer different types of input.

Some people provide strong emotional backing; others focus on tangible forms of support, from the intellectual to the logistical to the financial. This is why it's important to have a wide network on which we can call.

Type Rs also pick and choose when and how to leverage support. We find a balance between trusting our own judgment and knowing when we need outside input, what kind of input, and to what extent it is useful.

In an age of interconnectedness as well as growing turbulence, many of our successes might rise and fall with our ability to leverage support. When our lives are in flux and we feel lost, our friends, family members, and colleagues provide reinforcement and validation. As we struggle to redefine ourselves, our support networks become that much more essential—acting as beacons to help us explore what's most meaningful in our lives, share our challenges and triumphs, and inspire us to reach for our goals and spur us to action.

Active Engagement

As Mahatma Gandhi once said, "The future depends on what you *do* today." Such is the case with Transformative Resilience. TR takes place when the Type R mindset and its various characteristics and skills are combined with forward motion.

Active engagement is a matter of confronting our challenging experiences and emotions and choosing appropriate paths forward. This applies to both the actions we take and the emotions we invest in. But, it also applies to the decisions and interventions we make in the world, whether in business, relationships, community life, or politics.

Being actively engaged allows us to course correct and discover productive ways ahead after stress and challenge. It also creates possibilities that didn't exist before. If much of what we think and believe comes into question, we can be more open to new ideas, information, and means of doing things. In many respects it is an extension of hope. As we talked about in Chapter 3, hope is not an abstract notion. It enables action, propelling us toward our goals. It allows us to turn our visions for the future into a reality.

That said, we often find very quickly that facing adversity and setbacks can become overwhelming. One of the most common responses is the impulse to spring into "action" without gauging what's most needed. Who doesn't love to "fix a problem" and have an outlet for extinguishing the discomfort, helplessness, and uncertainty we feel?

In experiments with rats, neuroscientists in China and Taiwan found a significant difference between lab animals that were prevented from taking action to cope with stress and those that were allowed to act. When animals were strapped to a board without any physical means for coping, their physiological stress response and secretion of corticosterone, the chemical that regulates the immune and stress responses in rodents, increased to seven times the level from before they were restrained. The rats that were given an opportunity to cope through physical action, in this case by chewing on wood, did not have an increase in stress hormones above the baseline.[20]

When something goes wrong, people frequently want to react as opposed to respond. There's an important difference. Scientists get at the heart of this difference when they talk about our fight-or-flight response—the pounding heart and dizzy feeling, the knot in the gut that demands we react then and there to protect ourselves in the face of perceived danger. But physiologically and psychologically, a slower and more measured response can be more productive, especially when we're not in imminent danger.

It calls on different neural pathways and includes reasoned judgment that weighs action. It's the "take a deep breath and take time to think more clearly" type of response. With it, we can move beyond an initial fear-based reaction and draw on more nuanced signals and cues to harness our reasoning powers. Action begins with an assessment of the circumstances and the resources we have, both physically and psychologically. If we believe ourselves to be well equipped, we're more likely to engage and see the circumstance as a challenge. On the other hand, if we believe a situation calls for resources and abilities that extend beyond our own, we are more likely to perceive it as a threat and withdraw or become avoidant.

Research shows that those who focus on the challenge dimension of a stressful circumstance, rather than seeing it as a threat, experience a different form of stress. Their fear reaction is suppressed and instead a response linked to hormones and parts of the brain associated with positive emotions and learning are triggered, thus encouraging engagement.[21]

Both individuals and groups have a tendency toward being avoidant or actively engaged and toward reactive or responsive action. In some instances, they're able to engage in certain dimensions of the challenges they face, but not in others. For instance, Akira initially engaged with the stresses he faced and responded to his circumstances by moving across the country to look for work. But for years he avoided confronting his emotional turmoil and instead reacted to different situations on the basis of those unresolved issues. When he did engage on the emotional front, he found that he attracted greater opportunities personally and professionally.

Those who process and embrace the challenging circumstances and events in their lives as well as the resulting emotions with introspection, self-awareness, and a faithfulness to their core values are more likely to successfully embark on a path of constructive action. They take steps toward their goals that embracing hope allows them to set.

Consider the case of the city of Dallas, which we discussed in Chapter 3. It appears that after the assassination of President John F. Kennedy the city's leaders and residents collectively struggled with what had occurred. They reacted by blaming themselves and they avoided engagement. "Everyone in [that] tragic locale behaved as if denial was the preferred coping mechanism," University of California, Davis, professor Dean Keith Simonton said. "Dallas did not carry out the public observances that, through the proper choice of symbolic expressions, would have performed the needed group therapy for [its] citizens," he concluded.[22]

Yet years later, in the face of a new tragedy the city collectively engaged with the tragic events and sprang into action in emotional, intellectual, as well as physical ways. Citizens chose the kinds of events and conversations that would instigate change and be most productive in a time of mourning and heightened tensions.

Whether we engage in active coping or avoidant coping significantly shapes the outcome of the situation and our ability to transform difficult circumstances into meaning, innovation, and newfound strengths. Sometimes active engagement is our natural response, and sometimes it's a conscious choice, requiring what the Dalai Lama, the spiritual and political leader of Tibet, calls emotional hygiene. Emotional hygiene gets at the heart of being comfortable with uncertainty and letting go of our attachment to specific outcomes, which can cloud our ability to see situations clearly.

Emotional hygiene involves reining in negative feelings such as anger, frustration, fear, shame, and envy, which can impede progress and positive reframing. Especially during turbulent times, we must be attentive to our emotional state and avoid letting our emotions run rampant, overwhelming us, impairing our judgment and creative thinking, and inhibiting our ability to progress. Doing so enables us to more quickly move beyond our stress, discomfort, or pain.

Please keep in mind that this in no way negates or replaces the need to acknowledge and work through emotions like grief, especially in the face of loss and major change, or the need to seek professional support following major disruptions and crises.

That said, one of the biggest challenges of emotional hygiene is avoiding rumination. On one hand, appraising and re-appraising events can be helpful; rumination is also a way to feel in control and to avoid taking action by trying to "think our way out" of a situation. However, researchers have found that if re-appraisal goes too far without action, it leads to a downward spiral.

It's easy to get stuck in rehashing all of the things that have gone wrong. For this reason, an important aspect of active engagement is a focus on what's going well in our lives or our work while we also acknowledge the challenges. Returning to Jill, when she was struggling with what would come next in her career, she began to keep a journal of the things she was grateful for. This allowed her to shift attention away from her worry and doubt to what was going well.

"Th[e] process of staying very conscious about how much I had to be grateful for, how lucky I was even when I was unemployed—how privileged I was and how many great things I had in my life made me think that really no matter what it was all going to be okay—and that in fact it really *was* all okay," she says.

* * *

Transformative Resilience and the Type R mindset allow us to move away from a tendency to catastrophize and see circumstances in a problem-solution dichotomy that leads to mindless reaction or paralysis. Type Rs differ from others in the face of challenge because they can reframe circumstances. In the process of assessing our circumstances, we're more likely to believe that we have the necessary resources for growth and learning. We are then less likely to view adversity as a threat, which makes actively engaging seem significantly less risky because we believe we will experience a positive gain of some sort, regardless. We also have confidence in our ability to positively influence the outcome or to know when circumstances are beyond our control. This allows us to act by either making a thoughtful choice or by redirecting our energy in appropriate ways.

When we don't like where our lives, work, or circumstances are taking us, as Type Rs we find the means to change direction. We assess the situation and our resources, make the necessary adjustments, and then put a plan in motion. This involves calling on our core values and beliefs to guide us toward our desired destination.

Type Rs are aware of the high costs of avoidance and inaction. As a result, we rule them out as options because they can increase our anxiety or further inflame the situation. Failing to take corrective action in a timely manner or alienating others can create secondary crises and challenges.

The more that we as Type Rs become comfortable with engaging with what's in front of us and can face the emotions attached, the less likely we are to evade projects or people we find challenging or stress inducing, hoping they will disappear. We are also less likely to dodge distressing life situations by binging on Netflix and video games or overfilling our calendars so that we don't have to feel the discomfort.

Although Type Rs do appraising and re-appraising, we attach it to forward motion and a hopeful outlook. When we are actively engaged, we are better prepared because we anticipate challenges, scan the horizon for new opportunities, and adapt our responses to what's most appropriate.

Type Rs understand that growth is not only possible but critical at the times when we are most afraid, uncertain, stressed, and stretched. But growth depends on integrating learning into our outlook, which manifests in our habits and the steps we take toward our goals, large or small. TR is not possible without active engagement and a forward trajectory. We must take into account what we have been as an individual, a leader, a business, a family, or a city or nation and what we're in the process of becoming.

Today our individual and group successes and failures are more intertwined than ever before because of globalization, social media, and migration, among other things. With this in mind, together we must cultivate our ability to be actively engaged as we work toward the fruitful path that hope sets us on.

As discussed, we live in an increasingly demanding time, one that stirs us on emotional, intellectual, and physical levels—sometimes with a breeze, sometimes with gale force winds. The world constantly requires us to readjust as it changes beneath our feet. We must learn to adapt, mobilize our inner strength, cultivate clear judgment amid the uncertainty, change, and stress that we face both personally and globally.

But we also live in a time in which many of the challenges we face can't be tackled alone. We have to rely on our larger community—our support networks—not only to survive but also to truly thrive. There's a reason political slogans like "Yes *WE* can" have resonated across America and the world. They ignite our hope in parallel with our recognition of the need for sweeping change in ourselves, in our communities, and in the way we conduct business.

That recognition starts with a journey—one that may seem daunting at first, particularly given that we're often blindsided and catapulted into it by uncomfortable, if not painful, circumstances. But with the support of the Type R mindset and skills and the ability to harness the power of the storms on the horizon, we can travel to places brimming with promise.

CHAPTER 5

Transformers: The Type R Individual

It is never too late to be what you might have been.

George Eliot

IN THE EARLY 1960s, gangs carved up the Bronx neighborhood where Sonia Sotomayor lived. Muggers and addicts populated the stairwells. Tourniquets and glassine packets littered the sidewalks. It was hardly the place for a child to thrive, and yet it was home to the girl who would become the first Latina justice in the 225-year history of the US Supreme Court, and only the third woman to serve on the high court.

In 1962, she turned seven and was diagnosed with juvenile diabetes. At the time, having type 1 diabetes meant a dramatically shortened life expectancy. To her family, "the disease was a deadly curse," Sotomayor recalled. In her memoir, she describes listening to her overworked mother and alcoholic father fight over who would give her the daily injections of insulin she needed. "It then dawned on me," she wrote, "if I needed to have these shots every day for the rest of my life, the only way I'd survive was to do it myself."[1]

So, along with her morning routine of getting breakfast and brushing her teeth, she'd pull a chair up to the stove and boil water to sterilize a syringe and needle, measure carefully, and inject herself before leaving for school. "There are uses for adversity, and they don't reveal themselves until tested," Sotomayor explained. "Whether it's serious illness, financial hardship or the simple constraint of parents who speak limited English, difficulty can tap unexpected strengths."

Not only did Sotomayor overcome a difficult childhood while living with a chronic disease but she used the experience to transform herself into the strong and persistent woman we know today. Her adversity inspired an adaptability and a self-reliance that proved invaluable in her fight against racial prejudice. She overcame the odds and attended Princeton University and then Yale Law School. These traits were instrumental throughout her career in the New York district attorney's office, as a lawyer in private practice, as a judge in state and federal courts, and ultimately as a Supreme Court justice.

She credits her experiences as a woman and a Latina. "Few aspects of my work in the DA's office were more rewarding than to see what I had learned in childhood among the Latinos of the Bronx prove to be as relevant to my success as Ivy League schooling was," she said.

Through the years, Sotomayor has transformed her life and devoted herself to doing the same for others. In 2005, she recruited judges to join her in inviting young women to the courthouse for the long-standing "Take Your Daughter to Work Day" tradition. She also mentors young students from troubled neighborhoods. Being a role model, she said, "is the most valuable thing I can do."

* * *

When we hear stories like Sonia Sotomayor's, we assume that she must have been born as someone who has "it"—that elusive set of qualities that allows people to grow and use difficult experiences to their advantage.

Yet, Transformative Resilience is forged *through* adversity, not in spite of it. Stressful life events, disruptive change, and misfortune can bring out the best in us as we rise to meet the challenges.

Research has clearly shown that we are *all* born with at least some capacity to be transformed by difficult times. More importantly, research has determined that these traits of Type R are not static qualities. We can develop these behaviors throughout our lifetime. Type R isn't an either/or skill set. It's a continuum, and regardless of where individuals fall on the continuum, they can *always* increase their abilities, often as a result of specific events or mounting pressures coming to a head in ways that force change.

At these moments, a person can choose to grow and increase TR by actively and intentionally undertaking what we call the TR Journey. Although this is our starting point as individuals, the changes we make ultimately have lasting effects on how we approach and contribute to our personal and professional relationships, how we conduct business, and how we think of the challenges we face. Whole groups—families, businesses, communities—can also embark on the TR Journey.

The TR Journey

Wendy R. Anderson, whom we met briefly in the previous chapter, was twenty-nine years old when the Twin Towers fell, killing thousands of people in the September 11 terrorist attacks. Those terrible events led her to pursue a career that afforded her the opportunity to influence US foreign and defense policy. Within a few years, she had worked her way up and was living her dream as one of the only female senior advisers in the mostly male US Department of Defense. But it was a high-pressure environment, and she worked sixteen- to seventeen-hour days, six days a week, and was on call on her day off.

For nearly two decades, Wendy felt like she was doing the only thing she ever wanted to do with her life. But then she began to have doubts. She would wake in the middle of the night questioning the choices she had made. Her oldest friends started to give her honest yet hard-to-hear feedback. They told her, "You don't seem well," "You're tired all the time," "You're saying that you need a break, that you have no patience," "You seem tight and your leadership style is taking on those qualities."[2]

Wendy heard the warnings but found it hard to get off a path that she had been on for so many years. She continued to forge ahead at the same pace, rising ever higher into the senior levels in defense. Then she was offered an important promotion. The new job as chief of staff to Penny Pritzker, at the time the head of the US Department of Commerce, would be demanding and in an entirely new area of government, but Wendy accepted it all the same.

Before starting, she took a trip with friends to climb Mount Kilimanjaro and found herself enjoying the ability to shift her attention to a different kind of challenge than those that she was used to. The hike along with the company of friends and the sweeping mountaintop views allowed Wendy to start reflecting on her life in new ways.

"It was the first time I could see the tight, impatient, demanding, almost autocratic person that had developed as a result of a lot of pressure over a lot of years," she says. "I didn't like who I was . . . turning into. It was the first time that I could see clearly the feedback that people had been giving me."

Although Wendy had had inklings prior to the trip, during this time away she realized that she shouldn't have accepted the position at Commerce. But, not one to shrink from a challenge, she thought that if she just pushed and applied the same grit she always had, she could pull off the new job successfully.

However, within four months she found that she wasn't well suited to the role. A combination of a leadership style that didn't sync with the department's culture and the cumulative stress and fatigue from her years of working in high-powered positions led Wendy and her boss to conclude that the job wasn't the right fit. Wendy also decided it was time to leave government and put her years of experience and her talents to use doing something new.

Stepping away from what had been the driving force in her life was painful and disorienting. "The loss of that identity came in such a way that it made me reflect on all of the other life decisions that I hadn't made," Wendy says, pointing in particular to the issue of having a relationship and children. She had wrestled intensely with those questions. But this was the first time in her adult life that she took the time for this level of self-reflection. She insists that she wouldn't have done it if she had not been in what felt like a period of free-fall.

Wendy had a history of not listening to her own needs despite her growing exhaustion. It was as if she had spent years not fully taking stock or being honest with herself. "I acted as if 'I don't have limitations.' . . . And it wasn't true," she says. After leaving her job at Commerce, she finally was able to accept the fact that she did have needs as well as limitations. As a result, she started to shift her priorities to include her own well-being and focused on next steps for her career.

In the months that followed, Wendy spent a great deal of time at home reflecting. She talked with trusted friends and mentors and looked for support in various other ways to try to gain an understanding of why she was so upset and had personalized the events that led to her leaving the Department of Commerce. She came to understand that what she was going through was necessary, that it had to happen for her to move forward. She admits that she needed a wake-up call to force her to recognize where she was in her life.

As Wendy emerged from this particularly challenging time, she knew that she needed a more unstructured environment to rediscover her creativity, find new types of collaboration and new ways to exercise leadership, while also making room for friends, family, and a personal life.

While most people would take the logical step of returning to an established career, Wendy chose not to do that. Instead, she transitioned into the film industry, where she has become a partner in a media production company, creating a series of films highlighting the stories of American servicemen and women who have been in Iraq and Afghanistan.

Wendy has now chosen a life where she can be more open and can continue her commitment to national security issues, drawing on her previous experience and extensive roster of contacts, but in a far more creative way than she was able to do while in government. "It has been extremely transformative for me and I'm still in it," she explains. "I feel that I have been living more deeply in myself and who I am because I'm not living with the same inner conflict. I'm proud of what I've done."

* * *

Change is difficult even in the best of times. But as Wendy found, unforeseen change is even more challenging, especially when it is initiated by adversity or stressful life events.

Throughout history, stories have shown us that people, even in vastly different parts of the world, grapple with common themes. Among the most compelling are the stories of men and women who have been thrust into a journey of change by challenge and adversity and who come through the experience transformed. These tales reach back to the beginning of many religions and spiritual traditions, each with their own version of metamorphosis, from Buddha's to that of Moses and Jesus. To this day they remain a tradition that we draw on in popular culture, from Harry Potter to Luke Skywalker.

These stories help us understand the common path that so many of us travel and how to use our experiences to become stronger, more confident, and capable—in other words, how to be Type Rs and find Transformative Resilience in our lives and work. In studying these patterns, we have identified six important stages for turning adversity into growth that we call the TR Journey. Although we focus on individuals here, these are stages that groups, whether families or organizations, often go through as well, and you will hear such echoes in the stories in the chapters to come.

Stage #1: The Comfort Zone

Each of us finds our place in the world. We allow ourselves to be defined by the structures and systems we've put in place, from our job titles and accomplishments, to our partnerships, families, and the houses in which we live. We fall into habits that allow us to operate without having to think through each of our daily decisions; our habits become part of who we are. This equilibrium, whether ideal or not, is self-perpetuating and so far-reaching that we fail to notice it. We're at home in the world we've created for ourselves.

Scientists point out that there are evolutionary reasons we settle into these habits and routines. They save us time and mental energy.[3] We can take neurological shortcuts that guide us through our day without expending significant amounts of brain power to process the constant stream of information coming at us.

Additionally, because one of our primal needs is for security and stability, we equate familiarity with safety. Consequently, we're drawn to what we know. Our brains reason, "Hey, we've tried this before and it worked out. So it's probably safe to keep doing it."

It may not necessarily be the best way, but it's something we know. It's how we've always done things, even if the results are limiting, outdated beliefs, or dysfunctional behavior. We rely on the stories we tell ourselves and learned behaviors to keep us within our comfort zones. We may make small changes, but we largely stay within the safe boundaries we've created. Often, we can't even imagine any other way of functioning. We're inclined to ignore signs that change is coming or is needed. For Wendy, the story she told herself was that she could keep pushing and pushing to the point of exhaustion. It was the voice telling her, "This is what we do and who we are" that kept her in a challenging but familiar place.

Stage #2: Disruption

Change is one of the only things we can count on in life, and it often comes in the form of disruptions that shatter the familiarity of our comfort zone. It shifts the balance, and we realize that nothing will ever be the same. Change, stress, illness, and a range of other disruptions may sneak up on us gradually or overwhelm us like an earthquake that shakes us to the core, shifting the ground beneath our feet and reverberating into the future. What was once familiar, comfortable, and solid no longer exists.

A disruption can be anything from the very personal, like a relocation, divorce, or loss of a loved one, to workplace commotion, such as a sudden organizational restructuring, a loss of a key client, or a work burden or stress level that becomes unmanageable. Or it can result from global events that find their way to our door, because of a financial crisis, a terrorist attack, or a natural disaster.

Disruption threatens the stability of what we've relied on. Most people initially resist the changes that a disturbance demands by denying its validity, avoiding the issue, or blaming someone for causing the problem. We struggle to maintain life as we've known it and cling to the way things were.

People often retreat to protect themselves and channel their energy into taking stock. When our lives are disrupted, there's a sense of disbelief. We may say, "Yesterday he was here, today he's gone. How can that be?" or as Wendy said, "When I started this career, I was so enthusiastic and energetic. How can I feel so burned out now?"

We mull over the situation, trying to make sense of what's happened, and search for some semblance of control as we try to find a way to cope with the chaos. It's a time filled with confusion, anxiety, and stress.

We often become fearful and stressed about not knowing what the outcome of the disruption or change will be. And, it's not uncommon for us to feel helpless, depressed, and stressed during this time. As we recognize that a change is occurring, we often long for the days when the old ways sustained us. Yet, as scholar Joseph Campbell wrote, "We must let go of the life we have planned, so as to accept the one that is waiting for us."

Disruptions aren't all alike. Sometimes we courageously seek changes; other times changes find us. Disruptions can be simply aggravating, or they may be unbearable, influencing the extent to which we are launched into a period of chaos. And the way we experience a disruption often depends on our stage in life, whether we are leaving home to begin college, launching a career, or preparing to retire.

Stage #3: Chaos

Whether we feel positively or negatively about changes and disruptions doesn't alter the fact that they lead to a dismantling of things as they've existed before. We're forced to question our foundations and assumptions, turning our attention to who we are, what we believe in, where we devote our time and energy, and who we want to surround ourselves with. We straddle the abyss between the known and the unknown, at times wishing we could simply retreat to the familiar, but there's often no turning back.

In the midst of chaos, the foundations that were supporting us have come into question or have been shaken. It's a time of searching, uncomfortable and fraught with anxiety, with occasional glimmers of what could be in the future.

At this point, we're more focused on our own sense of confusion than with the reality around us, and our fears are reinforced by memories of the past or uncertainties about the future. Some people hunker down and pretend that nothing has changed. Others feel a sudden sense of urgency—a need to change everything as soon as possible. It's not uncommon for our emotions to be unpredictable, even changing moment to moment, day to day. However, it's essential that we force ourselves to pay attention to what's real rather than what's imagined.

"One of the things that I do with really edgy moments is that I take myself right into the center of [them], which is unpleasant but necessary," Wendy says. In her own period of chaos, she recognized that she needed to explore. "How in the world did I contribute to making this happen? I've got to be able to look at it. If I can't look at it, I can't grow. If I can't grow, I can't be better later. If I can't be better later, what's the point?" However unsettling chaos is, it is often a requirement for a new, stronger self to emerge.

In theoretical physics when current behaviors prove insufficient for the degree of change required, a system goes into stress and begins to deteriorate. What's needed to help that system or in this case an individual or even an organization evolve is a *second-order change*. Only when previous ways of thinking and operating are thrown into chaos can we find a solution at the next level that enables us to break free from the patterns of the past.

Chaos is an opening for creativity, innovation, and change. It forces us to find solutions to difficult situations. Although it may feel like an abyss, chaos is actually rich in information even if we cannot yet understand it or make sense of it. However, if we acknowledge the opportunity presented by change and stress, we're more likely to position ourselves for a positive trajectory.

Stage #4: Catalyst

In a chemist's laboratory even the smallest grain of a catalyst can create substantial change over an extended period of time. It doesn't have to be large to have a significant impact. A catalyst kicks off a process of transformation, facilitating the nature and the rate of change that takes place in interactions between different substances, while remaining unaltered itself. In some ways it's a bit like the pieces of charcoal that won't light in your BBQ until you add lighter fluid and—voila!—a fire bursts to life.

We have the sciences to thank for this concept of the catalyst, which we see widely influencing how we think about change and the ways that we live, speak, and conduct business. In our daily lives, often in the midst of chaos a catalyst emerges, sometimes in the form of an idea or a new perspective that guides us out of the mayhem and toward a new state of being. It may take days, months, even years for us to regain clarity. But eventually a catalyst emerges and brings with it an "Aha" moment that heralds a new awareness of possibilities and opportunities.

For Wendy, the key moment came when she finally acknowledged that she had needs that had gone unattended for years. She realized that she no longer wanted to live in a "pressure cooker environment." All of these insights kicked off a process that began to shape what came next in her personal life, her career, and how she contributed to the world.

Stage #5: Integration

Having found this new perspective, we start to experiment with who we are, what we believe, and how we operate. We master new skills and knowledge and incorporate them into our lives. While things are still uncertain, we experience a desire to learn and grow. And often a sense of creativity, hope, and enthusiasm re-emerges. There is a feeling of moving toward something new. But we also need a certain amount of time for trial and error and to integrate ongoing learning along the way.

When we experiment, it allows us to test things, question our assumptions, and come to understand ourselves and the systems that we have put in place in new ways. It provides us with an opportunity to try out novel ideas and approaches without having to worry about success or failure or a demand for immediate perfection. Innovations are introduced that change who we are and how we operate in the world. Any subsequent growth or development occurs on a new foundation, even if it builds on some of the elements of the past.

During this time, we make plenty of mistakes, and every now and then our progress falters. This is a time when we may need additional support. We can be frustrated when things fail to work perfectly the first time. And yet as we learn what works and what doesn't, we become more skilled and hopeful. Over time, what began as an idea becomes an ordinary state of affairs, and things continue to improve.

For Wendy, this means taking on consulting projects that allow her to work with teams in different ways and test out finding a new equilibrium between a personal and a professional life. It also means applying her skills and passion in new arenas and experimenting with working in different kinds of environments. "A right set of things have developed because the choice was to experiment and give myself space and time and to be willing to have faith somehow," Wendy says.

She is now gaining clarity and settling into filmmaking as well as more broadly leveraging the creativity of the entertainment industry to address pressing national security problems. What is clear to Wendy and others of us in this stage is that this period is about finding a new normal rather than finding the way back to how we once were.

Stage #6: Renewal

Nothing is more representative of new beginnings than the crocus, one of the first flowers to push up through the cold soil each spring after spending the winter hidden underground. When we finally come through hardship and a period of gathering our strength and testing out what we might become next, we reach a point when we feel comfortable in ourselves and in the world, even if both have changed. This renewal allows us to reengage with the world, but in a new way.

Only after we've come through stress or hardship and retreat are we ready to make the commitment to do things in a different way and view ourselves as new people. Although we maintain our core values, renewal involves new understandings, beliefs, attitudes, and—most of all—new identities.

For Wendy, working on film projects with active US service members has provided a strand tying together her past and her future and is a way to bring her previous world into this next chapter of her life. Her projects keep her engaged and allow her to have some coherence in her life. "The films have been key. Through the work on these projects I'm learning a whole new way to be. It still feels very experimental, but I'm at peace," she says.

As we regain a sense of confidence in ourselves and the knowledge and skills we've acquired on the journey, we begin to establish ourselves anew. The time for experimentation is over, at least for now, and we embrace the next phase of life.

* * *

As we emerge from the journey that change and challenge have sent us on, we are ready to move on to the next phase. Adversity is an integral part of life, and we will likely face it again. And yet, now we know that we can not only survive but also prosper, and so have a greater sense of self-confidence to embrace change and challenges in the future.

We face change, trauma, or stress to varying degrees in different parts of our lives. We may be comfortable in our family lives, while at work we're in chaos; or we have a catalyzing moment after a sudden breakup that helps us shift into a new stage in our personal lives. Our lives are rarely all of a piece. The TR Journey describes the process we go through as we are catapulted into substantial change. Yet life isn't always neat and orderly, and in some cases neither is our process of change.

And no two people's or groups' processes are the same. The depth to which we experience the TR Journey can be affected by the extent to which we were in a comfort zone before the disruption as well as the scope and nature of the disturbance itself.

However, what is common is that Type Rs often realize that it's important and necessary to seek professional help in different stages of our journey, whether to help stabilize a situation in the midst of or shortly following disruption and chaos or to find additional emotional, professional, or technical support as we make sense of what has happened, adapt, learn, and grow.

That said, by understanding the process of disruption and change, we can better identify our circumstances and emotions. As a result, we can choose more effective responses, find the support and resources we need, and turn unexpected and difficult experiences into opportunities.

Transformative Resilience and the Contagion Effect

The ancient poet Rumi turned the well-known expression of being a drop in the ocean on its head when he said, "You are not a drop in the ocean. You are the entire ocean in a drop." That's not to overemphasize our own importance. Instead, it's a reminder that both the struggles we face and the growth that we experience reflect those of the larger world and our contribution to it.

At the same time, there's merit in considering the impact of a single drop of water. By using adversity in our lives to promote growth, we both consciously and unconsciously influence the actions of a significant number of people. Each of us creates a point of impact that makes waves that ripple outward through our various spheres of influence.

When we capitalize on Transformative Resilience, we're doing far more than simply improving our own lives and well-being. The more we benefit as individuals from TR, the more everyone around us benefits. By creating changes within ourselves, we can impart the advantages of TR to our team, our organization, our families, our community, and even the political arenas in which we engage.

Seemingly insignificant actions and influence can have major unexpected impacts on the world. Though many of us can't see the ripple effects that we create, a growing body of research shows that, as Type Rs, we have the potential to affect a number of others through biological and social processes of contagion as well as through the power of persuasion and influencing.

When we hear the word *contagious,* we think of something that should be contained—a cold, a virus, a financial crisis. The phrase *emotional contagion,* which we still use today, was coined in the 1890s by German philosopher Max Scheler to describe the ways that our emotions and behaviors trigger similar emotions and behaviors in others.

The science of emotional contagion goes back to 400 B.C., when Hippocrates, the founder of modern medicine, observed that some women seemed to transfer "hysteria" to one another.[4] By the 1700s, researchers began to discover that people mirror the smiles and frowns they see on someone else's face. And by

1759, the Scottish philosopher Adam Smith, known for his contributions to modern economic thinking, observed that, as people imagine themselves in another's situation, they display "motor mimicry" or adopt the emotions of others.[5]

Contagion's cousin *influencing* first came into use in the 1500s. Yet, for centuries if not millennia humans have exercised the power and ability to compel or persuade the beliefs, mindsets, and actions of others through our own perspectives, arguments, actions, and decisions. Recent research that explores the role individuals play in social networks demonstrates that a good deal of our behavior is contagious: our habits, attitudes, and actions spread through an intricate network of connections to subconsciously affect those around us.

Our daily lives are filled with examples of how we "catch" subtle emotions from other people. Social scientists have discovered evidence that emotional contagion affects all human relationships, from intimate to business relationships and even to team sport.

Nicholas Christakis, a physician and psychologist, was working as a hospice doctor at the University of Chicago in the mid-1990s when he first noticed emotional contagion and the importance of social networks. He was struck by the case of one patient in particular, an elderly woman who was dying of dementia, and he noted the impact it was having on her family. Her daughter was depressed and exhausted from taking care of the dying woman. In turn, the daughter's husband was depressed and exhausted. But the event that triggered an insight into emotional contagion was a phone call that Christakis received from a close friend of the husband, who explained that he too was depressed and exhausted by the experience of his friend's wife and his friend as they took care of the dying mother. "Here I get this call from this random guy that's having an experience and being influenced by people that are at some social distance," he recalled.[6]

Contagion seems to involve both biological and social functions. It's prevalent, and yet we're often unaware of the impact of others' emotions and actions on our own—which is particularly striking because the consequences of contagious behavior can be considerable.

Biologists think that mirror neurons in the prefrontal cortex—the part of the brain involved in social behavior—are triggered and mimic the feelings and actions of another person, laying the foundations for contagion. We copy others instinctively.

Nicholas Christakis paired up with political scientist James Fowler and began to study the influence of social networks. Existing research demonstrates that people can "catch" emotional states they observe in others over time frames ranging from seconds to weeks. Given that they knew it was taking place, and often quite quickly, the researchers wanted to find out who most influenced people and how much their social proximity came into play.

In their study of 4,739 people and 12,067 social connections, Christakis and Fowler measured individuals' happiness through the use of surveys and tracked changes in their happiness over time by using their social networks. Ultimately, they found that an individual's satisfaction was associated with the contentment of people up to three degrees removed in their social network.

On the basis of this and other happiness research, they suggest that this contagion applies more broadly to emotions like depression, anxiety, and loneliness as well as behavior affected by those emotions such as drinking, eating, and exercising.[7] This research provides the foundations for understanding that the emotions associated with TR and Type R are also contagious.

That said, Transformative Resilience and the Type R mindset also play an important role in influencing those around us, both near and far. We have all experienced how the emotion expressed in a powerful speech or how a public figure acts in the face of a tragedy can affect us despite a lack of direct contact. Is this emotional contagion, influence, or both? It may be fair to say that these close cousins work on their own in some instances and in concert in others.

Not all of the effects we have on others as individuals are delivered through contagion. We also have a great deal of influence through our actions and interactions. We find many examples in sports. Batting averages of teams in Major League Baseball show the influence that a player's performance has on teammates. When a batter follows two teammates who have hits, his success or hit rate is 50 percent to 70 percent higher than when he follows two batters who struck out.[8] Seeing someone else undertake successful behavior can help us replicate that behavior, whether it's hitting a home run or adopting a Type R mindset that encourages perseverance and learning in the face of failure, stress, adversity, or loss.

That said, while contagion is passive, influencing is often a process of exercising the power of persuasion. Influence is transmitted in how we communicate our beliefs, perspectives, knowledge, and experience. And in some cases, we simply act as a role model, whether consciously or unwittingly.

In the same way that we fall into habits or use stereotypes to help us take shortcuts we use our connections to others to sift through all the information we take in. The behavior of those around us helps us decide how to act, from choosing a doctor to how we conduct ourselves at work or respond to a crisis.

Social validation or social proof plays a large part in influencing: people are inclined to adopt a mindset or set of behaviors if they see that others—and particularly others they believe are like them—have done it. Take, for instance, the experiments of experts like Robert Cialdini and his colleagues. In one experiment with hotel guests, the researchers aimed to see what would most compel them to cultivate what might be characterized as Transformative Resilience through more sustainable business practices.

In each hotel room was a sign asking guests to reuse their towels to conserve water. At the start of the experiment, most guests already did reuse their towels part of the time during their stay. But the researchers wanted to find out how guests were influenced by one another. The researchers made two sets of signs and placed them in a series of hotel rooms. The first placards had a simple conservation message to the effect of "please recycle your towel to help us save water." The second set of signs suggested that the "majority" of hotel guests recycled towels during their stay. Given the extent to which we are social animals and influence one another, it should be no surprise that the group with signs alluding to the behavior of others had a 26 percent higher rate of recycling towels than did the other group.[9]

Following the crowd isn't simply a matter of being a lemming or keeping up with the Joneses. Social scientists point out that it speaks to three underlying human motivations: to make accurate decisions as efficiently as possible, to affiliate with and gain the approval of others, and to see oneself in a positive light.

Influence in the context of individuals can take many forms. It can be as simple as unknowingly influencing a friend to seek out continued learning through our own example or it can be as complex as convincing our team at work to take a new approach or to reframe a crisis. It can even reach the heights of global politics and business. The notion that we as individuals are too small to instigate change simply isn't true.

In particular, we don't think of the very young as being influential. But consider Malala Yousafzai, who at age eleven began an extraordinary path of influence. She shared her example with the world through her blog, which she wrote from her native Pakistan. Yousafzai hoped to study to become a doctor despite the Taliban's unrelenting attempts to intimidate her and other girls away from obtaining an education.

Her determination made her a target of the Taliban and led to an attack in which she was shot in the head. Years later, in 2014,

Yousafzai was the youngest recipient to accept the Nobel Prize. Standing at the podium, she humbly told the crowd, "Some people call me the girl that was shot by the Taliban. And some, the girl who fought for her rights."

Her path to recovery, reframing, and growth as well as her continued advocacy for girls' education clearly identify her as the latter. Yousafzai is an immense source of inspiration for those near and far whom she has continued to influence as she advocates for a world in which all children are educated and girls have equal opportunities to fulfill their dreams.[10]

But Yousafzai's story also reminds us that influence is often a combination of factors. Among them is seeing the example someone sets, being able to relate to or empathize with someone, relating to a person's social standing as a trusted or recognized source of information, or being moved by someone's ability to inspire us with their vision.

There's tremendous power in not only asking people to change but also providing an alternative vision and lighting the path toward it. Someone's passion for something can be inspiring. For instance, employees who work from an inspiring vision can better convey enthusiasm or confidence once they succeed in making a particular change or making it through a difficult period or project. We can inspire change so that others want to be part of it.

The Power of Transformative Resilience

Whether through contagion or influence, when Type Rs cultivate Transformative Resilience it creates a ripple effect and sparks change in others. When we exercise a greater awareness of our emotional responses and choose to make healthier choices that allow us to move away from anger, frustration, or feelings of defeat and toward hope, optimism, and confidence, we transmit these positive emotions to others.

We all have significant potential to influence with our TR—to persuade others with the personal choices we make, the new visions and ideas that we present, and the ways in which we model new behavior. In a world in which everything is interconnected and rapidly changing, none of us has absolute control over anything, perhaps with the exception of our own mindset and perspective. But that in and of itself is more powerful than futile efforts to control events and the actions of others.

The closer personally and physically we are to others, the greater the potential for contagion and influence. Or we might proactively introduce new perspectives using our stature among colleagues, a group, or community to influence.

When others see us find a better path and ultimately succeed and grow, they're likely to be convinced of the merit of the ways we have reframed our challenges. They might notice the subtle or sometimes drastic shifts in our emotional states, the reordering of our priorities, how we choose to spend our time, what information we seek, or what solutions we find when life doesn't go to plan.

What's Your Type R Quotient?

As we thought about Transformative Resilience and how we can bring these skills into the different areas of our lives, we developed this assessment to help you understand your Type R abilities. It will help you evaluate your areas of strength, what needs closer attention, and what you can contribute to your spheres of influence.

Answer each question by choosing Very Much, Mostly, Somewhat, or Not at All according to which answer applies to you most frequently. If you aren't sure, ask yourself, "How would my best friend or loved one answer this question about me?"

	Very Much	Mostly	Somewhat	Not at All
Adaptability				
I have an ability to accept changing and difficult circumstances and in doing so adapt, reframe, and find positive outcomes.				
I have the ability to use the right resources at the right times to adapt.				
I am able to change course and choose new strategies in response to shifting demands and circumstances.				
I am able to think laterally and consider new options and ways of doing things.				
Healthy Relationship to Control				
I am confident that I'm able to influence some of the basic elements of my life.				
I acknowledge that there are external factors that affect me, some of which I cannot control.				
I have a strong sense of when to exercise control, when to persevere, and when to let go and channel my energy elsewhere.				
I have overcome a significant stressful or challenging event previously and believe that I am able to overcome new challenges in the future.				
Continual Learning				
I regularly evaluate my understanding of myself, the situations I encounter, my surroundings, and the world I live in.				
I reflect on the lessons that I can extract from the hardships or stresses that I experience so that I can be prepared for new challenges.				
I am curious and recognize that the more I learn, the more I desire to learn.				
Sense of Purpose				
I have a sense of meaning in my life that contextualizes my experiences (e.g., dedication to family or making a contribution to my field of work).				

	Very Much	Mostly	Somewhat	Not at All
Sense of Purpose *(continued)*				
I use my values as a compass—these values keep me on course regardless of the confusion or challenges I face.				
When facing adversity or change, I am able to find deeper meaning in it despite chaos, stress, worry, or despair.				
My sense of purpose or deeper meaning in my life provides a reason to aim for something and move forward when faced with adversity.				
Leveraging Support				
I have a network of strong social support that I can count on in times of trouble both personally and professionally.				
When confronted with adversity, I am able to overcome embarrassment about facing challenges and reach out to a trusted circle of supporters rather than isolate myself.				
I have a good balance between trusting my own judgment and instincts and knowing when I need outside input.				
Active Engagement				
I trust that no matter what happens, I possess the inner resources to cope and engage with the changing circumstances in my life physically, mentally, and psychologically.				
More often than not, my tendency is toward confronting and engaging with challenges rather than being avoidant.				
When something goes wrong, I take the time to consider the root causes and my ability to influence the outcome, and I respond rather than react.				
In the midst of stressful circumstances, I acknowledge and accept my emotions while reining in those negative feelings that can impede progress and positive reframing.				

The more often you answered Very Much or Mostly, the more Type R you are and the more Transformative Resilience strengths you have. Although IQ and EQ (emotional intelligence quotient) both play a role in success and life satisfaction, your TRQ is critical in times of disruptive change.

Keep in mind that other variables, such as your age, gender, and cultural and social values, influence your answers. That said, this is an important starting point for understanding your mindset, foundation, and skills.

No matter who we are or what our abilities are today, we can always increase them tomorrow. Transformative Resilience is an endlessly renewable resource that we can call on for everyday challenges, such as making time for our children while managing a demanding career, or grappling with the overwhelming difficulties that confront the world.

CHAPTER 6

Navigating Uncharted Waters: The Type R Leader

A leader takes people where they want to go. A great leader takes people where they don't necessarily want to go, but ought to be.

Rosalynn Carter

INDRA NOOYI, CEO of PepsiCo, doesn't fit the traditional image of a leader. She calls her mother in India twice a day and occasionally walks the halls barefoot, singing—a throwback to the girls' rock band she was in as a teenager. But we mustn't be quick to dismiss the woman who guided Pepsi through a number of rocky years and is at the heart of its re-evaluation and new approach.

When Nooyi was tapped to lead Pepsi in 2006, she was the company's first female CEO. She had already been with the company since 1994 as a strategist and had advised it to sell off portions of its failing fast-food chains. She had then moved on to being chief financial officer and doubled the company's profits.

But as CEO, she realized that much larger changes were needed. Pepsi had to adapt its business to reflect and take advantage of the changes occurring in the world. And it needed to become more socially aware and a better global citizen.

Consumers were becoming more health conscious. Obesity in the United States was increasing at alarming rates, tripling in adults over the previous three decades, rising sharply in children, and growing in countries around the world. Limited natural resources also posed increasing challenges for Pepsi, which was denied permission to open plants in certain countries with limited water resources. And the issue of plastic waste was a growing problem.

Instead of competing for more market share in a quickly shrinking soft-drink industry, Nooyi looked at the bigger picture. As she reframed, she realized that the fundamentals of the way the company made money needed to change. "We needed to move to a model that had transformation at its very core, in line with the changes of the world," Nooyi explained in 2014.[1] "We needed to embed it formally into our culture." This required a different kind of thinking and a new set of priorities, leading her to develop a global strategy that focused on sustainable practices while accelerating long-term growth.

Nooyi knew Pepsi had to address increasing global concerns about diet, obesity, and health and restructured the company's portfolio so that healthy options like juices accounted for 20 percent by 2013. Under her guidance the company also set targets to reduce the sugar content in its products and was able to remove 434,000 tons by 2015 in the United States and Canada alone.

She also realized that emerging economies' growing consumer power and cheap production capacities meant that they had to rely less on the West as the exclusive driver of their business and profits. Pepsi also needed to be aware of social issues in the countries where it operated and to undertake water-saving efforts in places such as India and deal with waste issues, seeking innovative solutions such as making plastics out of plant-based waste from its products.

That's not to say that everything has gone smoothly. Wall Street investors and the media criticized Nooyi heavily for placing too much focus on healthy products, which, they believed, caused the stock price to decline. A recent advertisement aiming to portray "unity and understanding" in a divisive US political context misstepped and garnered significant criticism. And the fact remains that health problems are linked to snack foods and sugary beverages, and many corporations, including Pepsi, must continue to grapple with the social, environmental, and economic footprints of their businesses.

Nevertheless, many of Nooyi's strategic decisions are gradually beginning to bear fruit. Consumers are proving Nooyi right in her decision to focus on healthier products. Annual net revenues had grown to $63 million in 2015 compared to $35 million in 2006. The company also estimates that it has saved $600 million between 2011 and 2016 through water, energy, packaging, and waste reduction initiatives around the world.[2] And Nooyi has gained a reputation as a forward-thinking leader.

"The rapid change and volatility that [have] defined recent years [are] only going to accelerate. That will require unusual, innovative solutions. . . . In other words—constant transformation," she explained in an interview.

She also emphasizes that much of the potential for growth in an organization stems from leaders like her first changing themselves and then bringing those strengths, skills, and insights into the organization. "I cannot just expect the organization to improve if I don't improve myself and lift the organization," she said.[3]

Some of the greatest challenges she's faced lately, though, come from within her organization. In the divisive environment amplified by the recent US presidential election and spikes in racism, sexism, and homophobia, Nooyi has grappled with how to support her employees in difficult times. The question her employees are asking, especially people of color, women, and LGBT people, is, Are we safe? This is something that Nooyi never thought she would have to address.

And yet she's in a good position to empathize with her staff and tackle some of these issues. She is part of a new generation of leadership in which more women and people of color are taking the reins and beginning to understand the importance of their experiences and their roles in an increasingly diverse but also turbulent global context.

One of the key tools that has helped her through a number of challenges is reframing experiences and not assuming that she immediately understands other people's intentions. For Nooyi, the key is truly investigating others' perspectives and identifying the underlying sentiment and needs rather than reacting negatively. This stance changes what could be confrontational or oppositional interactions into productive ones. She's also an avid reader and continually learns about and seeks out new social and business information that helps her contextualize differing perspectives and steer the business in what she thinks is the right direction.

Many call Nooyi a demanding leader, and she sleeps far less than is feasible for most people. But, as she juggles these internal and external challenges, she reminds herself that one of the most important parts of leadership is staying human and relying on the support of others while also trying to provide it in times of uncertainty. "Don't forget that you're a person," she concluded. "When your job is done, what you're left with is family, friends, and faith."[4]

Recalibrating the Leadership Compass

To be a leader in the twenty-first century isn't to control or avoid challenges; it's to learn to find our footing regardless of the circumstances. It's not a matter of bouncing back when we fall or falter. It's about growing from the experience no matter how challenging it is in a way that allows us to be more sure-footed, yet humble. It's about being better equipped for the next challenge and the one after that, while embracing those experiences and using them to build greater strengths and prepare for the future.

The World Economic Forum and Harvard University point out that a large number of the issues that keep business and global leaders up at night are those that affect society as a whole, ones that are both local and systemic, persistent, and with causes and cures that are hard to pinpoint such as climate change, scarcity of water and food, poverty, cyber-attacks, not to mention the world we are leaving to our children. To solve these problems requires that we depart from the status quo in ways that are particularly uncomfortable and that require us to equip ourselves with a new set of skills.

It's no surprise, then, that many of the most successful leaders draw on a Type R mindset as a foundation for enacting a different kind of leadership that allows them to embody Transformative Resilience and contribute it to teams, communities, and the larger world. Leaders with Type R skills and behaviors increase their own abilities so that they're healthy and effective and can model good behavior and balance the varying demands they face.

Together, this mindset and skill set also help leaders navigate the challenges of organizational cultures and internal dynamics, from crises in employee engagement to retaining talent, harnessing diversity, and aligning the organization's values with the way it carries out its business. And, given the immense uncertainty in the world, this new way of thinking combined with increased know-how informs the way leaders conduct business and engage with the outside world. They cultivate TR as they chart a path through challenges and unforeseen shocks, whether they are related to financial crises, shifts in markets and competition, shrinking global resources, or increasing social and political tensions.

The more complex problems become, when they spread beyond the ability of a single person to solve, the more the nuanced guidance of Type R leaders is required to adapt to and prosper in changing times.

Type R: The Sure-Footed Leader in Changing Times

Today heads of various companies and organizations have lower success rates and shorter tenures; leadership turnover in business hit a fifteen-year high in 2015.[5] Over the last decade this has resulted in part from leaders' egos and lack of emotional intelligence as well as their being out of step with a changing world. It's understandable, then, that people around the globe increasingly believe we need a different kind of leadership.

To determine which qualities were most important for leadership today, social sciences columnist John Gerzema and journalist Michael D'Antonio surveyed sixty-four thousand people in thirteen countries. The team first identified traits people generally considered masculine, such as competitiveness, egocentricity, and decisiveness, and feminine, such as adaptability and cooperation, before surveying to determine which qualities were most important for leadership today.

What they found was that many of the most valuable leadership traits overlap with what people identify as more "female," collaborative characteristics that both men and women can demonstrate and that are key elements of the Type R skill set.[6] They include flexibility and openness to people with differing perspectives, an inclination toward continual learning, and the ability to leverage networks.

The core belief that we have the capacity to cope with and grow from the challenges we face forms a solid foundation for leadership that, combined with the six Type R characteristics, enables leaders to address challenges and draw on their ability to continually learn and engender the support of others. From here, leaders have the potential for imparting Transformative Resilience to others and tackling complex business and global challenges in more effective ways.

Other factors also play an important role in leadership. Among them is the capacity to embrace uncertainty, see new experiences as opportunities for learning, and remain anchored by a strong sense of purpose.

Type R leaders have an internal compass to guide them along with the ability to develop a clear, multifaceted perspective, relying on Type R Vision, which we explore in more depth later. These leaders adapt to what's needed at a given time. From one day to the next, this means reminding employees of the organization's mission and purpose, providing a sense of stewardship, maintaining productivity, or inspiring colleagues to adjust to new realities.

Leaders often do this by offering fresh perspectives and resources while encouraging innovation and creativity. Type R leaders make wise decisions by channeling their efforts into progress rather than into controlling factors that are outside their grasp, uniquely positioning themselves for success in turbulent times.

At the same time, Type R leaders are ideally suited to motivating change in others. Research shows that leading people through difficult times is usually a matter of challenging what they hold dear—asking them to give up long-held beliefs, habits, and loyalties.[7] Given how difficult this can be, employees and colleagues want leaders who inspire and help them rise to the occasion and accept change and new realities.

By cultivating a positive mindset, leaders transmit TR to their teams, their businesses, and their organizations and among their peers. As philosopher Albert Schweitzer said, "The three most important ways to lead people are: . . . by example . . . by example . . . by example."[8]

Continual Learning and New Capacities

We as leaders go through different stages of development, teaching others as we continue to evolve ourselves. That development is significantly influenced by how we view our skills and ability to continue to grow. It also reflects how we understand and relate to the outside world and the events taking place around us.

A significant amount of the stress that we as leaders face today has less to do with workloads and more to do with the challenges of trying to make sense of an environment that has become too complex for our existing stage of leadership development.

A number of technical skills help managers and directors with jobs in specific sectors, and that's most often where the leadership path begins—having excelled at a technical level. The key to becoming increasingly effective, according to experts at the Center for Creative Leadership, is shifting the way that we think rather than continuing to add large amounts of technical information to an increasingly full "vessel," but one that might not be the right shape or properly oriented. A shift toward thinking in terms of complexity, systems, strategy, and interdependence, combined with technical ability, is far more likely to be successful in today's world.[9]

"Many of us have either been taught to be leaders or have experienced leadership as what has been coined as 'expert' leadership. 'I'm the boss. I know everything,'" says Joanna Kerr, a senior leader who has been at the head of organizations such as Action Aid International, a poverty alleviation charity that works in more than forty countries. "It's a 'top-down' approach and it's very common . . . as opposed to co-creative leadership, which is crowd sourcing and is a much more twenty-first-century idea."[10]

For Type Rs, leadership is facilitative, open, inclusive, and reflects a shift in the level of skill and mindset. It also includes paying attention to power dynamics and what's taking place at the margins. After all, it's frequently at the periphery of organizations and groups where innovation takes place, and that's also where there is the most inequality.

Failure and crisis are two of the best catalysts for growth and acquiring new skill. In fact, research has found that ongoing success stunts the continual learning process fundamental to Type R leaders. This is partly because we're less likely to spend time analyzing our success and properly pinpointing or attributing its sources.[11]

Immense shocks, whether triggered by failure or other challenging circumstances, help us stretch and expand our thinking and, as a result, our leadership skills. After interviewing 150 CEOs at large corporations across countries and industries, researchers at University of Oxford's Saïd Business School concluded that crisis is a key factor that enables leaders to successfully reinvent themselves and grow because it disrupts their identities and old patterns of behavior.[12] Growth stems from a mindset that says, "We have been through hardship before and, should it occur again, we will be able to make it through, learn from it, and better ourselves." This makes us more effective as visionaries, managers, and strategists.

For Joanna, the catalyst for change came in a very personal and devastating way. In October 2005, two nights before she was to host a global conference in Bangkok as executive director of AWID, an international women's organization, she received a shocking call from her sister.

Their father had committed suicide. There was no warning, no preexisting depression. He was just gone. "He was the parent of unconditional love.... When my dad died it was that kind of heartbreak that you don't even know is possible," explains Joanna in our conversations with her. His suicide shifted the tectonic plates beneath her, and the event split her life into two parts—before and after.

But, perhaps surprisingly, the death of Joanna's father was particularly instrumental in helping her become the leader that she is today. It affected how she functions as a manager and has contributed to the skills and perspectives that she brings to the teams and internal cultures of the organizations that she has worked with. It has deeply influenced how she approaches complex problems and global challenges.

"To have that kind of pain and then to be able to carry on day by day and continue to care for myself, my family, and the organization that I was running at the time . . . in hindsight gave me a courageousness and a belief in the power of the human spirit," says Joanna. The experience significantly increased her belief in her ability to chart a path through and grow in the face of difficulties of all kinds.

It also helped Joanna become more comfortable with uncertainty, enabling her to learn and develop new skills, both in spite of and because of the volatility around her. After having survived the most devastating kind of disruption that could have taken place in her life, she was able to put other kinds of disturbances in context, which made them feel manageable in comparison.

A starting point was handing over responsibility for the AWID Forum to her colleagues and enabling them to take charge even though she had led the planning for months. This was a particularly difficult decision given that the organization at that time was so closely tied to her identity as a dynamic and visible leader. Learning to relinquish control made Joanna a better, more inclusive leader who enables others to assume responsibility. She also learned to leverage the talents of people around her so that she could focus on the bigger picture.

After experiencing a loss of this magnitude, Joanna also became more comfortable with the pain and stress of others. Leaders with empathy model good behavior and allow others to find effective, compassionate ways to support one another. All of these are important factors of Type R leadership—the belief in the transformative nature of challenges, the confidence built by facing adversity, the capacity to face disruption and the discomfort of others. And these are particularly powerful when combined with a larger vision of the mission and purpose of our work.

Adjusting Our Perspective: Type R Vision

So much of good leadership is about having an overarching, big-picture perspective. A significant portion of what we as leaders do comes down to our vision and our ability to translate it into action and to gain buy-in from others.

Vision is about how we understand the landscapes around us, whether geographic, social, financial, or political. It's a matter of how we process information through various lenses and communicate that vision within our organization and to our key stakeholders. It also reflects our internal values and sense of purpose and the ways in which those guide the goals we set and the choices we make.

It's for this reason that one of today's most important tools for leaders is what we call Type R Vision, a powerful combination of four key elements: (1) agile framing and reframing, (2) the ability to balance the micro and the macro perspectives and have foresight, (3) the ability to perceive the speed at which challenges unfold, and (4) a multifaceted perspective.

Agile Framing and Reframing

As we know, our understanding of any given situation depends on how we frame it, where we place our attention, and the mindset with which we approach it.

When we reframe or reposition our perspective, things may look significantly different. According to psychologist and Nobel laureate Daniel Kahneman, unless there is an understandable reason to behave differently, most of us reflexively accept decisions and problems as they're presented. As a result, we seldom have a chance to understand the degree to which our choices are influenced by our perceptions rather than by reality.[13]

A different way of thinking about reframing is like the viewfinders photographers use to help them decide where to focus their attention in a 360-degree view. Do we tightly focus on what's in front of us, blocking out the wider picture, or do we place the subject of our attention within its broader context to give it importance within a larger whole?

This ability to reframe and place circumstances in a wider context has been particularly helpful for Joanna. "[I've learned] as a leader to ask, 'If you see this as a crisis, how do I help you see it as an opportunity?'" she says.

Prior to our most recent conversations with her, Joanna had become the executive director of Greenpeace Canada. She mentioned that a key senior staff member had quit suddenly after a short time with the organization, creating challenges for the rest of the senior management team. Several staff considered this to be a full-blown crisis. But Joanna's history allowed her to step back and place the situation in a larger context in a way that has made it possible for her to work with her team to reframe.

Throughout a series of meetings, Joanna took responsibility for a hire that might not have been the right fit. But she has also reminded the team of more difficult circumstances that they successfully navigated, placing their predicament in a wider framing. Together, they have discussed whether their challenges also present opportunities; in this case, the opportunity for the team to take more responsibility for new strategies for public engagement instead of depending on a single dedicated staff member.

Additionally, she has turned the lens and focused her team's attention back on themselves and their strengths, which helps engender confidence and allay fears. It took longer than expected to find a replacement, and two candidates fell through, making it especially painful. At the end of the year, Joanna's senior colleagues expressed how difficult the period had been. But they also noted how the prolonged gap in staffing provided an opportunity for them to learn about this critical part of the organization together and to figure out the best new strategy for the organization to move forward. Although they had to make do, the benefit was that both staff confidence and competence grew.

Near and Far, Present and Future

Most people joke about the day that they'll have to or already had to get bifocals, the eyeglasses with split lenses that fortify vision both near and far. And yet, metaphorically speaking, they may become one of the most useful items for the decades ahead.

Seeing what's immediately in front of us provides only a limited view of any given situation. The external environment in which we live and work is constantly changing, as are the internal dynamics and factors that we have to address. One minute something is a minor concern, the next it can erupt into a crisis. Add to that the power of modern tools like social media, and the scope and scale of challenges can change quickly. Type R leaders must be able to see into the future, too, to prepare for weathering gathering storms.

Continually evaluating a quickly changing external environment and understanding the kinds of disruption and risk we face and when they will become more of a threat—a kind of bifocal view of the present and future—are critical to TR. Greenpeace as an organization had to learn this concept the hard way, but it is one that is increasingly factored in to how it operates. In 1976 Greenpeace launched a campaign against the commercial hunting of seal pups used to make fur coats. The campaign took on a life of its own and became global, rapidly widening to a boycott of all seal hunting.

This led to a US ban on seal products and a European ban on products originating from whitecoat seals, among other repercussions. As the issue snowballed, it not only affected the fur industry but also created disastrous effects for Inuit subsistence hunters in Alaska and the Arctic.[14] The average income of an Inuit seal hunter in the Nunavut region of Canada plummeted within a year of the ban. The Inuit blamed Greenpeace.[15]

Decades later, Greenpeace is still healing the rifts left by the role it played in those events, despite the fact that there have also been additional campaigns and legislation spearheaded by others up until present day. This is a reminder that we can't be sure what tomorrow holds or foresee all the impacts of our decisions, so we must be ready to adapt in the face of uncertainty. And, on the other hand, envisioning, researching, and projecting potential futures, an important tool that futurists have developed, can be employed on the path to Transformative Resilience. Type R leaders must learn to imagine possible outcomes and alternative realities to prepare for and perhaps better accept change when it comes. Although Greenpeace has learned this in hindsight, its experience offers lessons for present and future leaders about making amends for past missteps and viewing decision making through a different lens.

Speed and Timing

Understanding when to speed up and when to slow down is often the difference between good and bad decisions. Many of the most successful leaders are highly sensitive to quickly changing conditions.

Leaders assess risk and the need for change on the basis of how likely they think an event is to occur and the impact that they think it will have. But most of us often fail to take into consideration the speed with which different circumstances develop, partly because our understanding of risk can be constrained by previous experiences.

For example, estimation of the fluctuations of stock prices is set against the highs and lows experienced since the 1929 Wall Street stock market crash. For centuries, we have predicted potential flood lines according to the highest point floodwaters have historically reached. With the advent of technology that controls huge amounts of the volume of trading on Wall Street and in markets around the world, and with the impact of climate change, these models no longer have the predictive value they once had—think back to the 2008 financial crisis and the impact of hurricanes like Katrina and Sandy.

Occasionally, those at the helm have had to deal with a catastrophe such as a stock market crash or a major storm. However, now what all leaders face is the increasing speed at which events unfold and the fleeting risk or opportunity that they present.

Today what differentiates effective leaders is the capacity to deal with increasing amounts of volatility at more frequent intervals. To handle the speed at which risks and circumstances develop, we must acknowledge the limitations of our thinking. If the risks that we face are about to exceed or have already surpassed the scope of our previous experiences and the speed at which prior challenges have unfolded, we have to reframe to understand and measure them.

That said, a successful response to change, threats, and uncertainty is not a matter of devising the quickest solution. Type R leaders watch trends on the horizon as they develop. When disruption finds its way to our doors, we don't simply jump to react. We have already been anticipating unfolding events and challenges, considering their scope and scale and speed of development.

Think about Indra Nooyi. She watched the news about obesity grow into concern over the health impacts of sugary drinks and foods with high fat content. She saw the trends coming in advance. She noticed that reports were comparing the health effects of sugar to those of tobacco, that some schools were banning sugary drinks, and that some US cities placed a special tax on them. Because she saw these trends develop and gain momentum and speed, she had the time to test the market for healthier products such as fruit juices before scaling up market share.

This kind of vision enables us as leaders to gauge whether we have a chance to test different responses on a smaller scale before investing heavily in one approach or whether we have to respond quickly and make the best decisions possible with the information available at the time.

Multifaceted Perspective and Kaleidoscope Vision

As children, many of us had a kaleidoscope—an optical toy that when held up to the eye creates a collage of patterns and colors, almost like panels of a stained glass window, that continue to change as it's turned, and tumbling objects reconfigure and are reflected by the mirrors that line the inside. And yet, as adults, we often forget the curiosity that comes with a kaleidoscopic view and its constantly changing multifaceted vision.

As Type R leaders, we see multiple contributing external and internal factors and views and place our own perspective within that larger context. We see ourselves as one piece that contributes to the whole, like a single shard of color within a kaleidoscope or a single panel in a stained glass window. To see with this type of vision, however, requires practice. If unchallenged, the power that comes with leadership can blind us to the importance of the perspectives, contributions, and needs of others.

The work of a group of social scientists led by Adam Galinsky at the Northwestern University Kellogg School of Management highlights the challenges of empathy and perspective for leaders. The researchers conducted an experiment in which they gathered participants and split them into two groups. One group was given exercises that induced feelings of power. The other group was given a set of activities that emphasized their lack of influence. Then participants in each group were paired to do the "E test," which measures perspective and empathy. One person in each pair was asked to draw a capital letter *E* on their own forehead. If participants wrote the letter *E* so that it was backward to themselves but legible to their partner, they had taken the other's perspective. If they had written the letter so that it was readable to themselves but backward to their partner, they hadn't taken into consideration the other person's point of view.

Participants who were made to feel like leaders, or the "high power" group, were three times as likely to draw the letter oriented to themselves. In other words, participants who had received a small infusion of a sense of power became less likely to orient their perspective to someone else's point of view.[16]

One of the skills that helps counter the blinding effect of power is self-awareness, which is also a key factor in our overall leadership ability. By analyzing the skills of six dozen top business leaders and the outcomes of their approaches and initiatives, researchers at Cornell University concluded that self-awareness was in fact the strongest predictor for leadership success.[17]

A significant part of self-awareness is anchored in our ability to see ourselves, our importance, and our struggles, both at home and at work, within a larger context. And sometimes that awareness means understanding that we lack the necessary perspective and must seek it from others.

A decade after her father's death, Joanna says that one of the best outcomes has been her heightened self-awareness and ability to guide others to be more reflective about their perspectives, behaviors, and biases, as she and her team grapple with complex global challenges where people often have deeply held and opposing views.

"You can see how battles among [different] value systems are going on in our public discussions all the time. But if we as leaders could [listen] better to understand those things, we can go into our meetings and be much more fluent across all values, and we can appreciate and judge less about where the other is coming from," Joanna explains.

She adds that one of the greatest challenges for people, herself included, is letting go of ego or ideology to enable these conversations—an issue she regularly broaches with colleagues.

This difficulty arose just months after Joanna joined Greenpeace when she realized that the organization's ability to work effectively in the Arctic was hampered by the historic rift with the Inuit.

"I could empathize with their deep hatred of Greenpeace for being seen as having taken away some of their economic livelihoods . . . the way in which they felt that the organization and other animal rights groups stigmatized them as cruel to animals and how unfair that was," says Joanna. For this reason she wrote a public apology in 2014, which built on Greenpeace Canada's new policy on indigenous rights and acknowledging historic wrongs.

The apology required Joanna to truly embrace humility and approach the situation with the ability to be vulnerable and to honor multiple perspectives. It was one small step to try to heal a long-standing divide and the pain felt by both the Inuit and the staff of Greenpeace over the unintentional side effects of the organization's early seal campaigning.

Joanna explains that her team has had to navigate its relationship with other Greenpeace offices in different parts of the world that have differing views. But she and her Canadian colleagues in particular have tried to bring a spirit of generosity and humility to the conflict and a genuine desire to make amends for past injustices and misunderstandings, and to right the wrongs through the promotion of new economic opportunities for the people of the North.

One of the positive developments in this challenging process has been that the residents of Clyde River, one of Canada's northern Inuit communities, reached out to Greenpeace for support after reading the apology. The community was confronting the proposal of a consortium of Norwegian companies seismic blasting to find oil, which the community's Elders believed would endanger their marine mammals and local food sources. Greenpeace supported the community in fighting its case in the Canadian courts. And in July 2017, the Supreme Court of Canada unanimously ruled against further seismic testing in the area given the lack of proper consultation with the Inuit. Joanna acknowledges this is only the beginning of a new relationship between Greenpeace and the Inuit, but it's an important start.

Navigating entrenched conflicts and differing views such as these is no easy task, which is in part why leaders are interested in building new skills that help us focus and regulate our minds, become more aware of our egos, and allow us to become steadier in ourselves. One way that many leaders do this is by cultivating a mindfulness practice. Though they originate in Eastern philosophy, mindfulness techniques are not religious and instead focus on developing awareness of our thoughts by concentrating on breathing and building empathy for ourselves and others. These exercises interrupt the brain's counterproductive repetitive patterns as well as calm and steady the mind.

"Mindfulness has its roles to play in influencing [leaders], the way they conduct themselves in their day-to-day lives, making them more open, more compassionate, more empathetic, better balanced to face challenges and have an impact on policies and decisions that will be taken on globalization, on climate change, on the well-being of societies in the world," says Chris Ruane, when we sit down with him in London.[18] Chris introduced mindfulness training to the UK Parliament when he was a Member of Parliament. This work has had such a significant impact that Chris now works with leaders in government in over forty countries. And many top leaders, such as Aetna's CEO, Mark Bertolini, have also taken up their own practices.

Researchers and mindfulness experts point to the fact that many of the mindfulness activities, which increase our awareness of how we treat ourselves, in turn create a greater awareness of how we treat others whether they are near and dear or part of a larger society.[19] This awareness enables us to better take others into consideration while trusting our own insight during stressful times.

The Internal Compass

In times of crisis and change there's increased pressure to act quickly and, in doing so, to forgo our better judgment and defer to the perceived safety of following the crowd—the danger being a negative outcome. In fact, in a study that has now become famous, psychologist Solomon Asch showed that 75 percent of study subjects gave the wrong answer when surrounded by colleagues who also gave an incorrect answer, demonstrating the dangers of crowd mentality. Type R leaders, on the other hand, have a deep sense of purpose that allows us to adapt to changing circumstances and take in others' views while rejecting the pressure to conform in ways that aren't compatible with our vision, core values, and goals. We can channel our energy and guide others while staying on course.

Many think of purpose and the idea of making a contribution to the greater good as something that pertains mostly to "socially oriented" leaders. Yet, in a range of leaders from corporations to communities, many of the most successful ones define themselves by purpose and their ability to have an impact.

An overarching sense of purpose helps insulate leaders from life's everyday stresses and from catastrophic events. "With something larger in mind, something yet to be fully imagined, something to be looked for, then the hazards and the hopes, the trepidation and the triumphs of work are magnified and given import and meaning," wrote corporate consultant and poet David Whyte.

A vision and sense of purpose built on a set of unwavering core values also create stability, which is particularly important for those who depend on leaders in challenging times. It gives them the sense that amid change and chaos they can count on our core beliefs—a commitment to people, a belief in fairness, or whatever they may be—because those of us who are leading an organization, a process, a community, or even a nation are predictable and anchored in some way. By cultivating a sense of purpose along with the other Type R characteristics, we influence others through our outlook, decisions, and actions, and we inspire productive behavior in others.

Paul O'Neill, the former CEO of aluminum producer Alcoa, is a great example of how Type R leaders have used a strong sense of purpose and vision to create stability and harness the power of change, seeing it as an opportunity. After being hired as CEO, O'Neill shocked the company and its shareholders when he turned his attention to safety rather than the economic bottom line. He believed that safety could transform the company while making a profit.

There were ongoing injuries and deaths across a number of industries, including one at Alcoa just prior to O'Neill being hired. And, though on-site accidents in companies like this are tragic, economics often came first, dictating how business operations were structured. This overshadowed other values and led to business cultures that allowed for a certain number of accidents per year as a cost of doing business, according to O'Neill.[20]

But he was determined to prove that a truly great organization could be founded on values without reservations or excuses—for O'Neill, this meant making sure his employees were safe. He had observed early in his career that companies that focused on financials as their top priority were not very effective at other activities. If they instead were able to produce excellent results in other key areas such as safety, the financial results took care of themselves. Placing worker safety and people above the economics that structured the industry was in and of itself a form of dissent; he turned business logic on its head.

"I knew I had to transform Alcoa. But you can't order people to change," he said. In one crisis after another, O'Neill faced the issues head-on. In O'Neill's first year, another worker was killed in an accident, and O'Neill felt personally responsible. Rather than feeling discouraged that his vision wasn't translating into success, he recommitted to it and intensified his efforts. He knew he was on the right path and believed that he would ultimately be successful.

O'Neill took advantage of the window of opportunity for change that the accident presented and asked that Alcoa staff issue daily safety reports from around the world. He understood the benefit of creating disruptive change, not just harnessing its power when it arrives unannounced. And so he decided to shake things up by setting a goal of zero workdays lost to safety issues, which sent the company's employees scrambling to figure out how to meet such a lofty plan.

Setting a target of zero accidents sent shocks through Alcoa. But O'Neill believed that an important part of leadership is to create a crisis. "If you're really clear about what your values are, people will get out of your way. You may have a tussle, but people will not resist you about things that are right," he said, reflecting on how people across the company responded to his efforts.[21]

Ultimately, this approach paid off. When O'Neill left the company, it was five times safer to work at Alcoa than ten years earlier.

And the company's market value had increased from $3 billion in 1986 when he joined to $27.53 billion.[22]

The success of change agents like O'Neill depends on the extent to which they're able to communicate their sense of purpose and vision to achieve buy-in from others while also empowering others to help make that vision a reality. For Indra Nooyi at Pepsi, this has meant ensuring that her vision is understood in order to successfully bring others on board with the notion that an organization's business model can be better aligned with social changes occurring in the world.

At first people tried to dismiss the ideas as "corporate social responsibility." So, Nooyi had to repeatedly reframe and communicate that it isn't about how the company spends its money but rather how it makes its money. She presented the idea in terms that Pepsi's staff and board members understood, linking it to some of their existing frameworks. This allowed her to broaden financial performance discussions to include key issues such as diversifying the company's products to include healthy choices, tackling environment issues, and creating a work environment where people can bring their whole selves to work without hiding portions of their identities based on gender, sexual orientation, race, and so forth.[23]

When Harvard professor John Kotter studied change agents, he found that leaders and those undertaking change undercommunicated their vision by a factor of ten. By analyzing the emails and communications of a number of leaders and their employees about a change process over a three-month period, he was able to calculate the proportion of communication within the group that the change message constituted. He found that leaders conveyed their message ten times fewer than employees and team members needed to hear it to buy in.[24]

This enforces what we already know about Type R leaders: we need to repeatedly communicate our vision. However, as we see with leaders like Indra Nooyi and Paul O'Neill, it's not just about repeatedly sharing our goals but also ensuring that we have a strong, clear message and one that resonates with employee, board member, and team member concerns and that speaks to stakeholders' ideals.

O'Neill used every opportunity to convey his vision about worker safety, from the first opportunity that he was given to speak to the board and the staff after being hired. When investors tried to redirect attention, O'Neill returned to his key message and reinforced the idea that the safety of the people who made up the organization would be the source of prosperity for the company. By repeating this clear, simple, and powerful message, he was able to eventually bring others along with him. The daily safety reports became a focal part of internal communications and reiterated the vision for safety each day. In addition, O'Neill held conference calls so that employees could communicate lessons learned to others following accidents.

Ultimately, he was intentional in the way he communicated by focusing on his aspirations rather than maintaining the status quo and being as good as everybody else. "It's a lot more uplifting to say we're going to be better than anyone can imagine is possible," he said.[25]

Healthy Sense of Control

One of the greatest challenges for leaders is finding the right balance of control—remaining true to our sense of purpose and vision, staying focused and moving forward, while understanding that we can't control many factors and that it's counterproductive to try.

By age twenty-four, Frederick Hutson had completed a stint in the Air Force, from which he was honorably discharged, and had built several businesses. However, in 2007 he found himself in prison serving a four-year sentence after he made some poor choices with one of the businesses—distributing marijuana through his mailing and shipping company.

During his time in prison, his ability to accept the things over which he had little influence allowed him to redirect his energy toward what he could control. He turned his prison sentence into a self-taught MBA and an opportunity to lay the foundations for his next business, which transformed him into a successful young entrepreneur.

Shortly after his release, Frederick founded Pigeonly, a $3 million start-up that helps friends and family keep in touch with prison inmates. A database keeps track of inmates' whereabouts in the prison system, delivers photos to inmates from loved ones, and helps prisoners make affordable phone calls.

In an environment where inmates have almost no control over anything—from when they eat to when and how they can contact loved ones—Frederick had to work with his new circumstances and use them to his advantage. He intentionally focused his attention on all the things that he could control instead of those he couldn't, an approach that sustained him through his entire sentence. What he could control, he says, was the kind of person he would be when he got out of prison. He started by reflecting on who he was and what his strengths and weaknesses were.

He underwent a period of intense discovery and ongoing learning that ultimately led to the founding of his company and his successful leadership of that business.

"What you hear [in prison] is that you're not going to be able to do anything. You're told that you're not going to be able to amount to anything," he explains in conversations with us. But like many other successful leaders Frederick rejected the idea that forces outside his control or chance events would determine the outcome of his life or his efforts. "Just like my decisions took me down this road [that led to prison], my decisions can take me down a completely different road. I genuinely believed that my fate was in my own hands. . . . I could decide what my fate would be based on action and based on how I spent my time. The more I practiced it, the more I found it to be true. I found it starting with small things," he says.[26]

Business experts like Jim Collins point to the power of those small choices and consistently paced efforts to help create a healthy sense of control among leaders in changing and difficult times. Leaders have to accept that they have little influence over many factors, such as financial markets, customers, technological change, and the natural environment. But Collins argues that when leaders undertake what he calls the "20-Mile March," consistently pacing themselves with midlevel effort regardless of good or bad external conditions, they have a sense of control and focus that enables them and their teams to move forward despite uncertainty and disruptive change. The companies whose leaders adopted this approach performed ten times better than others, according to Collins's research.[27]

The key is harmonizing our belief that we can steer our lives with an appreciation for the importance of external factors and the number of things that lie outside our control. Researchers at the University of Cape Town and the Ashridge MBA program in the United Kingdom surveyed more than sixty MBA students and found that people with a strong internal locus of control often took on too much responsibility for themselves and events in the environment around them.[28] As a result, they held themselves responsible for every outcome, hindering their leadership potential and creating high amounts of stress for themselves. They were also less likely to trust others to be responsible or capable of taking on aspects of leadership.

In contrast, Frederick's experiences in prison helped him learn to accept the limits to the control he had and to direct his energy toward what he could influence, which has become critical to his success as well as that of Pigeonly. To start, as an African

American man who grew up poor, had a prison record, and didn't have an Ivy League education, Frederick didn't have the profile that many investors traditionally look for. These were factors over which he had no control. So, he focused on using his unique perspective and experience as well as his market research to his advantage. He ultimately targeted investors who saw added value in his background and drive to build tech products to solve important social problems and reach underserved communities.

Learning to accept what he couldn't control helped Frederick embrace risk and the inevitability of making mistakes and moving on quickly. By understanding that he couldn't control every outcome of the risks he needed to take, Frederick was able to advance the development of the business. "Every failure that I've had was expensive and painful. . . . [But] it would get me closer to the end goal," he explains.

By letting go of some of his grasp over the organization, he allowed for others to have agency and be responsible for their own choices. First and foremost, he made sure that he was transparent about the external risks of the business and the challenges of working in a start-up so that his employees could make an informed decision about whether it was the right place for them. This created a team that's committed to the vision of the company and willing to remain faithful through the company's ups and downs (which we discuss more in the next chapter).

Frederick also asks his employees to undertake important jobs without dictating how they're done. He allows his employees to innovate and have a sense of ownership over their work while trusting the work will be done well. The reward has been a high degree of loyalty from those who have chosen to be a part of Pigeonly. This has been one of the company's greatest assets and has allowed it to thrive and grow in the intensely competitive and turbulent world of tech start-ups.

A Fine Balance

With the challenges we face today, the conversations taking place in corporate boardrooms, start-ups, nonprofits, multilateral organizations, and even community town halls are converging. As leaders, we must strike a delicate balance. We have to maintain a clear, decisive vision while embracing varying points of view as we create a more inclusive, innovative, and engaged culture in a time when it's imperative that we motivate others to adapt to ever-changing realities.

The world in which we work demands that we not only increase the amount of expert knowledge we have but also transform the way we frame and approach leadership and the vision that we bring to it. This means constantly updating and building new skills, being agile and adapting as we gain new information, while strategically leveraging support.

From organizational culture to empathy and self-awareness, leaders like Indra Nooyi and Joanna Kerr walk a fine line between strong internal organizational cultures and mounting global challenges, calling upon their forward-looking vision to see both risks as well as opportunities ahead. Leaders like Frederick Hutson and Paul O'Neill are also a reminder of the extent to which we have to find an equilibrium between what we can and cannot control, taking advantage of the opportunities for growth amid challenges and uncertainty while relying on a strong sense of purpose to guide us and create an anchor for others.

To engage and build the partnerships necessary in our tumultuous world, we have to be humble, saying, "I don't have all the answers." This is a challenge to traditional leadership, which paints leaders as impervious and all-knowing, and requires a shift in thinking, both for leaders and those around them. It requires a certain amount of vulnerability and the ability to set aside our egos.

Part of that is recognizing that there are no perfect answers. We must piece together what works by experimenting, observing, learning from others, and innovating. Lessons learned from taking different approaches to complex challenges highlight the importance of leaders' roles in asking questions, prioritizing relationships over structures, and reflecting on rather than reacting to complex challenges.

"In a gentle way, you can shake the world," said Mahatma Gandhi, one of the world's greatest leaders. This emphasizes the importance of the actions that we each take and the snowball effect they have. Only by bolstering our foundations in Transformative Resilience and having humility can we as Type R leaders bring appropriate insight and skills to the ever-changing world to help steer the businesses, organizations, and communities that our world relies on for progress.

CHAPTER 7

We're All in It Together: The Type R Organization

Alone we can do so little; together we can do so much.

Helen Keller

MASSIMO BOTTURA, OWNER and world-renowned chef at Osteria Francescana, a restaurant in Italy with three Michelin stars, and his Japanese sous-chef Taka stood looking down at a lemon tart in utter disbelief. It had been carefully crafted to serve to the last customers of the day, and now, there it sat—broken, half on the counter, half on the plate, its filling splattered across the otherwise immaculate surface.

Sous-chefs have been fired for far less in fine dining kitchens, which are known to be immensely stress-filled environments, between their fast pace and demands for impeccable execution. Add to that the fact that, though Osteria Francescana was becoming successful, it had been through difficult times in previous years. It's no surprise, then, that Taka was mortified and worried as he looked at the broken pastry.

"Taka's face was vacant and pallid," Bottura recalled. After a few moments of staring down at the dish, however, Bottura's face lit up, excited by a new idea. He made a frame with his hands and showed Taka the potential that he saw. "It's beautiful!" Bottura declared with enthusiasm. "Let's make this again, as if it was [meant to be] broken." At first the sous-chef didn't understand, but he trusted his boss. And, most importantly, he trusted Bottura's vision—the notion of capturing the essence and tradition of the Italian countryside while being fragmented by the learnings of error and the vibrancy of modern art. Together they splashed the canary yellow lemon filling across a new plate like a Jackson Pollock painting and balanced jagged edges of broken pastry atop it, creating what has become one of the restaurant's most beloved dishes: "Oops, I Dropped the Lemon Tart."[1]

"I learned [that] in life to move forward you learn from mistakes," Taka recounted of his blunder that day. The dropped tart could have been an experience filled with shame and stress. It could have communicated to Osteria Francescana's staff, who form part of the thirty-plus-person enterprise, that mistakes were never to be made and that nothing less than perfection was acceptable if they wanted to keep their jobs. Instead, the experience helped create an environment of experimentation, learning, and growth.

This was particularly significant given the Osteria's early struggles. Bottura had first owned a local trattoria in Modena, a traditional town in northern Italy where he grew up. The restaurant served all the local classic dishes and was very successful. But Bottura knew that he had to continue to expand his horizons. In 1994 he left to apprentice with world-class French chef Alain Ducasse. When Bottura returned in 1995 with his American fiancée, Lara Gilmore, they sold everything they had and together founded Osteria Francescana, a significantly more modern venture.

As a child, to avoid being bullied by his brothers, Bottura used to sit under his grandmother's kitchen table as she rolled out handmade tortellini. It was there that he found his early inspiration for cooking and baking, as flour gently sprinkled down onto him and he managed to catch the occasional tortellini that dropped from the table.

Bottura called on these memories and began to combine them with imagination, experimentation, and his recent French training, forging inventive new creations from age-old recipes. The problem was that Bottura, Gilmore, and the Osteria staff quickly found that the locals in Modena didn't appreciate this new vision. For them, it was a betrayal of the local culinary traditions that had remained unchanged for generations.

Osteria Francescana was often empty and received terrible reviews from locals scandalized by its modernization of dishes like his grandmother's tortellini. Unless people warmed to the restaurant, Bottura was ready to walk away from the business. It was at this point that Gilmore urged him to give it just one more year. If at that point they didn't have a breakthrough, they could move on, knowing they'd given it everything they had.

Rather than conforming to the old ways and trying to be something that they would never be, they used their challenges as a source of inspiration. As the friction with the local community about their departure from tradition intensified, Bottura and his team became ever more determined to find a way to take the Italian kitchen into the modern world.

A 1997 trip to the Venice Biennale made Bottura think more about his ability to expand beyond the confines of tradition. One art installation in particular caught his eye—a row of life-like pigeon sculptures that sat in the wooden crossbeams of the building with a bird's-eye view of the more historical art below, and left a trail of droppings on it. The metaphor was not lost on Bottura.

This emboldened him to push culinary boundaries and add another dimension to the experience of fresh local ingredients presented in entirely new ways. Gilmore teased out the details of Bottura's new stream of ideas to more fully develop them and translate them into something that could be communicated to the team and captured in their cuisine. Splashes of color and mixes of textures began to show up on the plate. Now it was just a matter of finding the right audience who would appreciate this fusion.

One night in 2001 a car accident diverted Italy's most important food critic to Modena and the Osteria. Two days later *Espresso,* Italy's top news magazine, published an article with the headline "post-modern Taglietella." The reviewer expressed his remorse that it took him so long to find Osteria Francescana as well as the fact that the Modenese people didn't yet understand Bottura's vision for Italian food.

That article opened the world of gastronomic critics to the Osteria, and they flocked to the restaurant from afar. They saw something that they hadn't seen in Italy in a long time: a group of people willing to take risks. Just months later, the Osteria was awarded several prizes by *Espresso* and received its first Michelin star. The tide turned and even the locals began to take pride in the Osteria. Today, it is recognized by Michelin as the best restaurant in Europe. Chefs now credit both Bottura and the Osteria with bringing Italy into the twenty-first century.

* * *

Bottura and his team's accomplishments reflect how Transformative Resilience occurs in organizations as a collective Type R mindset that unites a group of people in their shared ability to reframe adversity and use it as an opportunity to learn, grow, and innovate. It provides them with the confidence to accept the changes and challenges that they face. And it allows them to collaborate to reframe, acquire new skills and knowledge, as well as take action in ways that strengthen their internal culture and their approaches to external-facing business and interactions.

Building a base of TR may start with an individual visionary or leader, but it can also be the result of several members of an organization or team responding to events and circumstances and introducing a shift in thinking to the group. Regardless, a handful of factors are fundamental to the success of organizations, even if they manifest in different ways.

First, the culture of any group reflects whether an organization has Transformative Resilience embedded in its collective mindset. Culture indicates whether there's a Type R environment that will foster and reinforce positive, productive behavior and responses. Second, leveraging the abilities of those within the group to enable the greater whole to function better and ultimately prosper is particularly important. Continual learning is fundamental to many of us, but it's particularly critical for organizations to translate learning at the individual level into shared understanding and development. Finally, many organizations find that acting to bolster Transformative Resilience in others not only contributes to the greater good but also cultivates and reinforces their own TR.

There's no one-size-fits-all answer to today's challenges and disruptions, which span the range of organizations, sectors, and cultures. So, how can we talk about organizations and Transformative Resilience using broad brushstrokes? From the small family-owned businesses to multinational corporations to not-for-profits, all are exposed to a plethora of mounting pressures. Even if they shared nothing else, stress, change, and disruption are unifying themes, as are some of the critical factors that enable them to draw on the collective Type R mindset, vision, and skills to create Transformative Resilience in their responses.

It's All About Culture

Recent research by Deloitte found that 60 percent of employers surveyed said that their employees are overwhelmed by today's rapidly changing work environment, but few know how to help their organizations and staff navigate these demanding times.[2]

If Type R in individuals is based on a mindset, in organizations it's about creating a shared culture that builds on a group's belief in their ability to grow and learn from challenge while uniting around a common vision, adapting to new realities, and shifting behaviors and practices.

Acknowledging the role that emotions play in shaping an organization's culture and environment is an important starting point. Do they poison the well or sweeten the water in terms of how people feel about the organization and their ability to stay engaged and face adversity? Emotions not only spread from one person to another, as we touched on in Chapter 5, but also influence group dynamics and therefore the culture and DNA of entire businesses and organizations.

When Sigal Barsade was teaching management courses at Yale University, she set up an experiment in which she separated students into groups and secretly planted one student in each to act out a different emotion: enthusiasm, hostility, serenity, or depression. The results were shocking. The actor had an effect at both the individual and the group level, influencing the others' willingness to cooperate, their levels of conflict, and their ability to effectively carry out the tasks given to them—in this case, a simulated exercise related to a salary negotiation.

The groups in which the actor seeded a negative outlook turned increasingly negative and low energy. In comparison, the students in groups in which the actor planted positive emotions were not only more positive as a group but also perceived as more competent and cooperative by themselves and others.[3]

The emotional tone of a group plays a large role in organizational culture. At the same time, the collective mindset influences the framework that organizations work within. A shared Type R mindset creates the foundation for embracing challenges as opportunities and catalysts for development and evolution. This provides the scaffolding for organizations and groups to integrate the Type R characteristics into the skill sets, decision making, and behavior of leaders, employees, and teams. It also allows for integrating key Type R elements such as adaptability, continual learning, and the ability to leverage the support and knowledge of others into structures, programs, and processes that help cultivate Transformative Resilience or reinforce and amplify it.

For EY, the accounting and professional services firm formerly known as Ernst and Young, undertaking a process of culture change has been a means of survival. It has also been a reflection of the collective belief that change and challenges can be used to further the advancement of one of the largest privately owned organizations in the United States. Though it's still very much a work in progress, creating internal change has been at the heart of the firm's strategy to face a number of global challenges and changes on the five continents where it has offices—staying relevant amid a quickly shifting and highly competitive landscape as well as meeting changing client demands.

EY has been in existence for over 150 years, so its history and accompanying culture run deep. But in recent years the senior leaders realized that the firm needed to use the challenges it faced to undergo a significant culture change across the organization. A number of economic failures, including the financial crisis, had occurred throughout the first decades of the twenty-first century. According to Michelle Settecase, a senior strategist who has worked with EY in the United States for more than eighteen years, regulators had grown skeptical of the ability of large professional service firms to protect against abuse or misconduct. As a result, EY needed a shift in culture to build greater trust with its stakeholders and ensure that the company had more to offer than just technical expertise.[4]

In 2013 the company hired Mark Weinberger, an EY tax expert with government experience in the Bush and Clinton administrations, as its new chairman. Under Weinberger, the company was rebranded and developed a new set of global goals called Vision 2020. The change that Weinberger instigated largely focused on a move toward a more collaborative approach that enables better solutions and professional services and distinguishes the firm through that culture.

Many of the change management and cultural transformation efforts have been about collaboration and creating better relationships and interactions between people in teams. The hope is that this will in turn produce better results, even if they may at first create uncomfortable circumstances.

In addition to becoming an organization that's more dispersed and that works across national cultures, the nature of EY's work is changing. In years past clients contracted EY's services for the company's significant technical ability. Now EY clients, as well as many other people in search of business services, want a "trusted adviser" more than an organization that is equipped with a narrow set of technical abilities. Clients expect soft skills such as communication, social intelligence, and collaboration to a much greater extent.

It's no surprise, then, that EY's leadership sees engagement of its employees as the key to the firm's profitability and that they're trying to find ways to support and meet the needs of diverse staff members. Diversity and inclusion experts in the organization point to the importance of EY's ability to share a vision and for its employees and leaders to know how they contribute to that bigger picture.

EY has undertaken significant efforts to bring people across the massive global organization on board with the culture change. Among other training initiatives, a particularly effective one in the United States is a game that the company has developed.

When we speak with her, Michelle explains that most people she knew grumbled about having to take time off of work for the training. But she found that, as people loosened up, they allowed themselves to be immersed in the experience and learn from it. The game was designed to break down barriers by building teams across rank and organizational departments and facilitating the imagining of what the organization's transformation would look like and how each person would take part. It walked each of the teams through questions and challenges to shift the groups' mindsets away from the confines of their roles and a narrow task-oriented mentality toward more collaborative approaches to collectively achieving goals.

"It may seem like a subtle shift, but it's inherent in the broader shift that we're trying to accomplish," says Michelle. "We can't just audit the books, we can't just fill out the tax forms. We have to help our clients understand in the context of their business, in the context of the market, and in the context of the globe. That's a very different mindset than just coming in and 'doing your job' every day and completing tasks."

EY has already seen the benefits of this more holistic approach to work with clients in a range of sectors as it shares with its clients insights on different kinds of risk, market expansion, and customer engagement to help provide context around the business itself. This depends on having a highly skilled, engaged, and loyal group of people to deliver these services.

Based on global surveys the firm found that a work culture that supports people's ability to find balance in their own lives, especially given the demanding nature of their work, was the top factor for retaining employees and was a strong factor in attracting new hires, particularly Millennials. And those who were working flexibly were more than 23 percent more effective in meeting their personal and professional goals.[5] An EY survey in the EMEIA region also found that when people were empowered to work flexibly they were 53 percent more engaged.[6] The organization has made an important start in this direction over the past five years.

And, as with all organizational shifts, change has to be embedded in the daily business and people processes, toward which EY continues to strive.

For example, while many organizations offer "scheduled" flexible work hours on certain days of the week, EY aims to take a step further to offer informal flexibility and to empower people to decide when and where they work and manage the demands of their jobs. The teams that Michelle has worked on are a decade ahead of others at EY in terms of working remotely and flexibly. This has given her more time to see the benefits of moving away from a culture that associates work with being seated at a desk for a certain number of hours.

"If I need to walk away and spend time thinking about an issue or a project that I'm working on . . . I can do it in an environment that helps me think creatively, that helps me [contribute] my best," she says. She's also found that, although she may work fifty to sixty hours a week, her flexible schedule allows her to manage her health and be there for important aspects of family life.

Michelle is convinced that this management philosophy provides employees with space to cultivate resilience in their lives. It also fosters loyalty and initiative, which in turn can drive overall organizational resilience because people are willing to go the extra mile and work through difficult times together rather than disengaging or leaving.

Having loyal and engaged people is the starting point for organizations to weather storms together. Another key factor is for groups, like individuals, to believe in their ability to withstand change and difficult circumstances and to use challenges to their advantage to respond constructively. When a group shifts to a Type R mindset, people are less likely to feel stretched beyond their capacity or overwhelmed by their circumstances and are more open to one another as well as outside resources and information.

If the culture of an organization is geared toward Transformative Resilience, the Type R mindset becomes a foundation for a shared vocabulary as well as a jumping off point for new kinds of analysis, capacity building, joint ventures, and initiatives. An organization's or a team's belief in its ability to be tested is also reinforced and shapes whether failure becomes a stumbling block and source of shame or is used as a learning opportunity.

But, as we have heard from individuals and leaders, sometimes old ways of thinking and operating must be challenged or disrupted to allow for the analysis and reframing that cultivates TR. Just as individuals are inoculated by some hardship and build confidence and new skills from it, so too are organizations. The key is ensuring that processes are in place so that shared learning occurs and the larger group finds meaning and lessons in events that enhance growth across an organization instead of in a few individuals.

Ultimately, everyone in a group contributes to group culture and the collective Type R mindset. Some proactively influence group culture with their proposals and views; others reinforce it with their support and adherence to what become norms. That said, Type R leaders at different levels in organizations are crucial to setting the tone. When we have a supportive and encouraging boss, our alignment with our team as well as the larger organization or group is significantly increased. Going one step further, this level of influence suggests, as we saw in the last chapter, that our bosses and organizational leaders also shape the mental framework and culture within which we work and therefore play critical roles in becoming Type R organizations and cultivating Transformative Resilience.

When the highest levels of leadership foster a mindset and a culture that embrace change as a source of growth, organizations can adapt and prosper. This starts with creating the space and the processes to identify existing mindsets and then introducing procedures and tools that can help break down barriers and shift those mindsets, particularly as they relate to acknowledging and reframing failure, adversity, and stress. It also requires continual commitment, forward motion, and action to turn goals into a reality.

At a time when the majority of organizations surveyed by Deloitte report a lack of engagement as the top threat to their business—second only to leadership gaps—a collective shift toward the Type R mindset, vision, and skills helps to create a culture that strengthens and engages employees in new ways. A culture of confidence and Transformative Resilience leads to new solutions and ways of working that are better aligned with the new realities organizations face.

Organizations and their leaders can also build TR among their ranks by acknowledging and supporting the needs of a diverse workforce and creating a culture that respects people's personal lives and identities. For example, a number of initiatives at EY are geared toward engaging and advancing women and what the firm calls "visible and ethnic minorities" as well as LGBT employees. While many companies initiate these kinds of programs, EY has gone a step further in key areas.

In addition to creating networks and bias-awareness training, EY advocates for the rights of LGBT staff and all LGBT employees and has extended additional benefits to them. EY joined a US Supreme Court filing in support of marriage equality. The firm's leaders are also taking a public stand in the United States on immigration equality for LGBT people. And EY was the first of the large accounting firms to reimburse LGBT employees for additional federal and state taxes paid on same-sex domestic partners' health and welfare, which it started offering as benefit in 2012.[7]

Maintaining, if not increasing, these types of commitments, positioning themselves as an advocate for equality, and holding to a moral compass will be a crucial test for corporations in the coming years. This will be challenging amid a landscape of increasingly intolerant political statements and policies as well as rollbacks of measures that protect female, LGBT, and ethnically and racially diverse workers.

A Type R culture that's accepting and supportive of different people's needs and identities encourages openness that further leads to employee loyalty and involvement, ensuring that people are more likely to be on board through the good and the bad and enabling TR. It also creates a foundation for addressing the changing needs of those inside and outside an organization so that they don't become a source of future discord, disruption, or crisis.

Harnessing People Power to Adapt

Similar to the way Type R individuals need to harness the support of others to help them move forward, so too do Type R organizations. However, organizations are a bit like the stone-age cars in the Flintstones cartoon. The foot power of everyone in the car is required to propel them forward. The larger the car, the more foot power required. This also means more buy-in is needed from the group to ensure that everyone contributes and heads in an agreed-on direction.

In 2003 General Stanley McChrystal was appointed commander of the US Joint Special Operations Command, a counterterrorism organization, and inherited a unit made up of US military personnel and civilians he had not hired nor could he replace. He quickly learned that people have to have a sense of shared purpose and feel that they're contributing to something worthwhile to get them involved and collectively moving toward a goal. "If you ask people what their vision is, it's not: 'Hey, I'm here cutting this stone.' It's: 'I'm part of a team building a cathedral,'" he explained.[8]

Recognition goes a long way to incentivize people and can be critical for keeping them involved and engaged even in the most difficult of times. Experts at McKinsey & Company found that talented employees responded better to nonfinancial incentives than to financial ones. Praise and recognition kept most of them engaged. Attention from leadership, such as one-on-one meetings, also made them feel valued, as did opportunities to lead projects and tasks that made important contributions.[9]

Younger people in particular are motivated by opportunities to build skills, contribute ideas to organizations, and assume leadership roles. And it's not just this kind of inclusion that strengthens the culture but also, as General McChrystal realized, people on the ground closer to a given situation, who often have better intelligence for making decisions than those at the top, especially in difficult times.

For instance, during the Iraq war McChrystal relied heavily on his sergeant major, a subordinate who was on the ground. He was able to go visit different parts of conflict zones and gather information more easily than McChrystal could. He didn't need to travel with the kind of entourage that was required for a more senior leader and so drew less attention and was more nimble. The sergeant major also had the trust of local people and could draw out information in a unique way and report back developments and concerns in different regions.

When we spoke to Tim Vogus, a professor of management at Vanderbilt University in Nashville, Tennessee, he emphasized that leveraging the most appropriate knowledge and skills in an organization is among the most important factors for resilience and ultimately growth. Yet, organizations have to have the confidence, which comes with Type R, that they will be able to weather challenges. This allows leaders to loosen control and be more flexible. As a result, problems and challenges flow toward those in an organization who have the greatest expertise or most appropriate information.

That said, it's not just about calling on the most experienced people within a group of similar thinkers. Leveraging innovators and dissenters is critical for Transformative Resilience and for the evolution of businesses, nonprofits, community groups, and governments alike. We might think that creating harmony and uniformity, especially in challenging times, would be important. But that, in fact, can be harmful when the status quo has contributed to stress and crisis or has impeded continual learning that would prepare a group to face new realities.

Psychologist Irving Janis was one of the first people to discover the limiting effects of what he called "groupthink." When leaders create organizational cultures where conflict, dissent, and alternative narratives or perspectives aren't welcome, groups tend to conform in ways that cripple them with homogenous or uncritical thinking.[10]

Groupthink also discourages dynamic thinkers and younger people from fully engaging in their organizations. For instance, in the annual survey that Deloitte carries out on Millennials and their satisfaction with their workplace, at least half of these young employees complained that their companies don't reward innovative thinking or the questioning of existing work methods, leading them to consider moving to other jobs.[11]

Under the immense pressure of budget cuts and increased demand for services, the British National Health Service (NHS), which employs roughly 1.4 million people, is attempting to shake up groupthink. The hope is that the institution will leverage the full benefit of its diverse people and enable innovative thinking and new solutions to the challenges it faces.

A 2014 NHS report called for activating "disruptors, heretics, radicals, and mavericks" and focused on people who have learned to "rock the boat and stay in it." One of the keys to change, it said, is to move to the "edge" of organizations for leadership to increase diversity of thought, radical thinking, faster change, and better outcomes. "The new economy's equivalent of the industrial assembly line will likely be some system that celebrates rebels. This will be an epochal shift in management thinking," said Celine Schillinger, a consultant and adviser to the NHS.[12]

After discovering that the financial cost of sick leave taken by stressed workers in the NHS is close to $2 billion per year, NHS management decided to test one of the more innovative approaches some of its "outside thinkers" introduced. A group of 204 staff members went through a several-week-long mindfulness-based cognitive therapy course.

This approach reduced stress-related and mental health–related absences from an average of fourteen days per year for each staff member to just three. Because the pilot was tracked so carefully, the NHS estimates that this new approach saved £109,000, or roughly $170,000 in 2014. This alone hasn't solved the systemic problems and related crises that flare up within the NHS, but it has been a successful step in what many throughout the agency say is a desperate need for innovative solutions and culture change that will buoy the staff's and the agency's Transformative Resilience.[13]

The NHS isn't the only one trying innovative approaches that protect and leverage the talent of its people while turning challenge into strength. The Cleveland Clinic in Ohio has developed a program called Code Lavender, a holistic health rapid response system for those on the verge of burnout. The program was originally designed for patients and their family members, and yet it quickly became clear that staff actually needed it most.

Through the program, a health provider who sounds a Code Lavender Alert is attended to by a team of holistic care providers within thirty minutes. After receiving treatment, ranging from massage to yoga and mindfulness training, the individual wears a lavender armband as a reminder to relax for the rest of the day. The program is particularly welcome given that almost half of all physicians experience burnout—a figure that places them at greater risk than any other group of American workers, according to research by WebMD.[14]

Forward Thinking and Continual Learning

Part of the stress that so many organizations and their employees experience results from the fact that the internal and external environments are constantly changing. One minute something is a minor concern; the next minute it can erupt into a crisis.

For this reason, Type R organizations have to develop the skills to scan the horizon in ways that build TR so they can adapt in anticipation of coming challenges rather than deal with unexpected disruptions and crises. As we showed with Type R Vision, this requires leaders at varying levels to take in information at both the micro and macro levels, some of it more general and some of it more specialized. Leaders must look at the human element of their business and internal cultures while also keeping an eye on the technological, economic, social, and environmental trends that might quickly change the landscape within which they work.

Information has to flow through the organization and be combined with learning from other pockets of expertise to create a 360-degree view. This prevents blind spots that might otherwise result in lost market share, obsolescence in the face of new technology, or loss of essential personnel.

Yet, no organization can predict all disruptive change. When it does come, many of the most successful companies have learned that knee-jerk reactions and rapid changes in response to crisis are not effective. Research at dozens of corporations carried out by business experts like Jim Collins and his colleagues agrees.

For many Type R organizations, success means accepting that they can't control the external environment and to some extent the diverse group of people on the inside, either. Nor can they simply rely on their existing know-how. They can, however, be prepared to harness the emotional intelligence and talents of their people, adapt to changing circumstances, keep a tab on mounting pressures, and imagine what the future might hold so that they can be prepared to the best of their abilities. It's difficult to do any of this without being curious and asking questions.

According to Steve Quatrano, a board member of the Right Question Institute, business leaders want people in their organizations to be more curious, more aware of what they don't know, and more inquisitive. The act of formulating questions enables us to identify and fill knowledge gaps in ways that drive ongoing learning.[15]

It's essential that those in organizations maintain their ability to continually experiment so that they continue to get better at adapting to change. In other words, they must become better, faster learners so that they're continually experimenting with different ways of doing things.

This is an essential part of the process of cultivating collective Transformative Resilience. If something goes wrong or there's a near miss, Type R organizations treat the failure as an opportunity to learn and make improvements. In his research in high-pressure environments with high-stakes outcomes, such as hospitals and firefighting, Tim Vogus concluded that, although technical or operational improvements are important, they're not the most important factor for an organization's or team's growth and resilience. Instead, it comes down to people skills and people's ability to learn.

Organizations must hire and train for interpersonal skills and then give people the opportunity to make use of those skills in terms of more intentional interactions and choices. But it doesn't end there. "One of the things that's important for sustaining resilience is people experiencing those outcomes of positive change," says Vogus. Rewards and positive reinforcement make people more willing to offer the additional effort that it takes.[16]

Pigeonly, introduced in the previous chapter, couldn't be a more perfect example of an organization that faced a rapidly growing external threat and used continual learning and the collective abilities of its staff to transform a crisis to its advantage.

The trouble started one weekend in 2016 when founder Frederick Hutson received an email flagging suspicious traffic from the organization's phone service providers. Pigeonly's service reaches people in eighty-eight countries, and by the time the company investigated a few days later, it found that someone had exploited a loophole in the online platform and set up hundreds of thousands of fraudulent phone accounts registered in countries from Cuba to Suriname and Japan.[17]

In a twenty-four- to thirty-six-hour window, more than two hundred thousand fraudulent accounts were created. Although Pigeonly's computer system hadn't yet approved these accounts, they had generated close to half a million verification calls placed around the world. In turn, this amounted to thousands of dollars in phone bills for the start-up.

By the time the scope of the problem was clear, the situation had become a crisis. Frederick and his team knew that they were in trouble when their phone provider wanted to fly out to speak with them in person rather than having a conference call.

"When I'm in some sort of crisis, usually the first thing I do is try to move the metric of time," explains Frederick, recalling his response to the situation. To buy themselves time to assess, learn, and respond appropriately, the team decided to temporarily cut off all international services to limit any further damage. But this decision wasn't without consequences, including a deluge of complaints from international customers. "We had to find a balance of how to solve this problem without alienating a portion of our customers," he recalls.

Frederick gathered Pigeonly's engineering team, and together they began to assess and brainstorm solutions, leveraging the input and talent of the group. But they also felt that it would be useful to learn from others, so they drew upon the experience of their phone providers and studied industry best practices for account verification, turning to companies like Skype.

While Frederick's instinct was to cut off all global calling services for the foreseeable future, by leveraging the know-how of his internal and external colleagues Pigeonly came up with a far better solution. They created stronger filters and internal verifications before the system would allow an external verification call for a new account, limiting their exposure to the same kinds of problems in the future.

It was a stressful time, and months later the company was still working with insurance companies to figure out how to manage the financial damage that had occurred. However, the business as a whole went through a significant learning period that was beneficial to its bottom line as well as its culture. It forced the team to experiment with different solutions and refine the technical side of the business. It improved their products and generated a significant amount of new business for people overseas with loved ones in prison in the United States. Customers have seen that Pigeonly's system is safeguarded and provides high-quality service equal to that of domestic service, and the word has begun to spread.

Of equal importance is the way in which the crisis transformed the organization. Until then, Frederick, as the founder, along with a couple of other senior staff members, had largely shouldered responsibility for the success of the business. But that began to change after the fraud incident.

"This [was] a big enough crisis that it could have really impacted the future of the company. It made us start thinking in a way that we didn't think before," says Frederick, pointing to the group's process of learning and transformation. In particular, the crisis provided impetus to reflect on why certain checks and balances or procedures were needed, which staff began to embrace and were able to participate in updating and revising.

Across departments, from the engineering to social media and sales teams, staff members became more vigilant about what was taking place in their part of the business. They paid more attention to detail. For instance, shortly after the fraud, an engineer found that an online coupon that had expired hadn't yet been closed out of the system and was being exploited by a customer, which they were able to address quickly. By catching minor issues that come up in day-to-day business, they have been able to reduce the risk to the organization and the chances that something small could snowball into a larger threat.

"It has made people take more responsibility for the organization as a whole," explains Frederick. "It's not 'I work here, I clock in, I go home.' It is more a feeling of this being 'our' business and everything that affects the business affects us individually and it affects us collectively. People have taken on vigilance and now share in the overall success of the organization."

Thriving Together

Artist Andy Warhol drove to the heart of our interconnection when he said, "Human beings are born solitary, but everywhere they are in chains—daisy chains—of interactivity." He further noted that the actions we take together are courageous and stretch us as we negotiate "a compromise between 'his,' 'her' or 'their' wish and yours."

The world we live in and therefore the fates of our organizations, businesses, communities, economies, and even our families are more interconnected than in decades past.

Researchers at the University of Virginia and the University of Washington business schools recently found that companies that did best after significant challenges were those that reframed the group's mindset and put into place strategies for how to proactively deal with adversity. But an unexpected finding that proved to be one of the most important factors differentiating companies that thrived from those that didn't was a focus on the greater good. The researchers had surveyed 140 businesses across a range of industries. Those that engaged with their wider community and took action that benefited a group beyond their own during hardship showed better growth rates over a five-year period, including during the 2008 financial crisis.

The notion that an organization's prosperity relies on the well-being of the broader community, economy, and environment has existed for many years. Long before it was acquired by multinational Mondelez, Cadbury, now the world's second largest confectioner, invested in infrastructure that supported its workers and created stability for them. The company believed that this was the right thing to do and that its business would prosper as a result.

In the late 1800s, the firm expanded under the founder's sons so that it had to move out of the city of Birmingham to the countryside. This move could have disrupted the lives of many workers and made their working for the company untenable. But in 1893 the company began building a model village called Bournville, which included 313 cottages on 330 acres, to ensure good housing for its workers within a reasonable distance of their work. The Cadbury family was particularly concerned about the health of their workers and promoted fitness and development of public parks.

Though the company was by no means infallible, its philosophy of facilitating the interconnection of social well-being and business success carried over into the culture. It affected everything from the way that Cadbury sourced raw materials from overseas to the way it treated employees and structured the business. Ultimately, the company gained the loyalty of employees and customers around the world and became a great national pride of the United Kingdom and its private sector.

David Croft, who worked for Cadbury for years before moving on to other large food chains such as Waitrose and Kraft, explained that much of what allowed Cadbury to sidestep or transform challenges over the decades was the organization's sense of purpose and broader connection to the community. David has watched a number of mergers and acquisitions at large food companies in recent years and the impacts that they have on employees, organizational cultures, and, ultimately, the business prospects of these brands.

"A strong sense of purpose and the core values of the business create resilience and retain a sense of direction that holds people together during times of change and [challenge]," he says when we sit down with him. What's important is ensuring that the reason for creating change links back to an organization's vision and that the ways that change is developed and delivered are authentic and reflect the values of the business.[18]

The reality is that for much of the twentieth and part of the twenty-first century a significant amount of business and organizational operations has been disconnected from global social trends and the effects that business operations have on communities around the world. Yet, now there is a resurgence of understanding that Transformative Resilience in the community is linked to the TR of businesses and organizations and their staff. Today, along with Cadbury, a number of companies are making positive contributions to society as a result of acting on their core values.

There's a significantly greater understanding that aligning internal culture and purpose with an organization's external business and modes of operating isn't only a benefit but rather a prerequisite for success. "It's a lot like nutrition and complexion—the inside is the outside. In the old days [businesses] had a reputation that they would try and put out there and it may not be true," says consumer trend consultant John Gerzema. "In today's world of information it's really [about] starting on the inside."

That includes everything from how happy people are at work and whether they are able to bring their whole selves to work to whether they believe in the mission of the company and whether it helps their development and that of the larger community. "That has external benefits in terms of everything from better products to better services, better innovation, better customers because people are more aligned. We see that great companies truly believe in their missions." In other words, the focus on doing good has made these businesses better able to thrive in times of market challenges, increasing competition, and global disruptions.[19]

Deloitte's Millennial survey has specifically investigated how this generation thinks about business's role in society. The noteworthy conclusion of the research: a focus on purpose and people is, for many Millennials, just as important as a company's ability to create profit. And this sense of purpose was one of the key factors that shaped which companies young people sought to join when they started their careers.[20] But it's not just Millennials who care about social issues. Mission-driven organizations have 40 percent higher employee retention rates across age groups,[21] and "business with purpose" is shaping a large number of consumer choices today.

Returning to Osteria Francescana, this connection and dedication to supporting a larger community has been part of its success. Chef Bottura and his team feel a large sense of responsibility for the tourism the restaurant brings to the region and the connections it has to the livelihoods of farmers and local businesses.

Increasingly, Bottura believes that, in addition to ensuring that the Osteria's guests enjoy good food, chefs and restaurants have an important role to play in social justice. He is involved in efforts to reduce global hunger and to build a school for chefs near his restaurant in Italy. "The people at the top have a mission to bring as many people up to the next level as possible. That can be done by culture and education. This is the greatest challenge we have right now," he explained at a culinary event.[22]

This sense of giving back is something that the Osteria and Bottura have put into practice time and again. In May 2011, two large earthquakes just nine days apart flattened houses and damaged churches in the region where Osteria Francescana is located. The earthquake damaged 360,000 wheels of cheese worth millions of dollars—one round of cheese alone costs $1,500. That could have been the end of half the Parmesan producers of the region. Because they are neighboring businesses and an important part of Osteria Francescana's group of suppliers and the broader community, Bottura and his team stepped in to support the Parmesan makers and revitalize their businesses. Working with the Parmesan association, Bottura proposed an online "dinner party" where people around the world cooked the same meal at home with a new recipe that would utilize the broken wheels of cheese.[23]

The event helped sell all of the damaged cheese and played a vital role in getting the cheese makers back on their feet and creating an even greater global profile and appreciation for the artisans of the region. Not one person lost their job or their business. Although the primary goal was not self-serving, the event also created a significant amount of press and attention for the Osteria and provided the restaurant with a resilient supply chain of artisanal local cheese and a strengthened community of colleagues.

The Way Forward

More and more we face failure, competition, disruption, and stress. Do we pick up the spilled tart and make something new out of it, as Bottura and his team did, or do we wither in the face of failure and stressful circumstances? More than ever, how we answer this question defines our ability to progress and thrive as businesses, organizations, and groups.

From Osteria Francescana's and Pigeonly's adaptability and willingness to learn to EY's overhaul of its business fundamentals, we've seen that a culture that draws upon and lays the foundations for further developing Transformative Resilience is a defining factor in taking a step forward and thriving.

Time and again culture and people—beginning with the people who bring a Type R mindset to the group and confidence in the team's shared ability for transformation and growth—are the drivers of success. Progress happens most when people collectively adopt a positive mindset and are willing to engage, reframe together, collaborate, and contribute their best in stormy weather. Like Pigeonly, Type R organizations are able to get people on board with change and harness their input on the most appropriate ways to respond to disruptive change and crises.

And as we have heard in this chapter, Transformative Resilience is closely tied to a workplace environment that celebrates openness, develops a culture of engagement, and values and leverages the knowledge and input of employees to enrich the diversity of ideas.

Though not entirely surprising, many of the Type Rs who are most successful don't go it alone. They become experts at reframing internally, but they also align their internal values with their interactions in the outside world. They strengthen their own foundations, TR, and ultimately business success through a deeper sense of purpose and by instinctively being a positive contributor to the broader ecosystem, treating others as part of a wider family.

While the notion that your success and well-being is closely tied to ours is not a new one, it's one that's proving to be more and more important for so many of us. We rely on others at work in ways that often replicate family dynamics, and much of our success on the job relies on the extent to which we find support and create Transformative Resilience in our families.

CHAPTER 8

A Bridge Over Troubled Water: The Type R Family

In every conceivable manner, the family is a link to our past, bridge to our future.

Alex Haley

ANGEL LE KNELT with his six-year-old son, Brandon, next to a mountain of flowers and candles left in memory of the young concertgoers who were gunned down in Paris by terrorists on November 13, 2015. In a video that has touched millions of people around the world, the young French boy, with a round face and big brown eyes, conveyed his fear. "The bad guys have guns. They can shoot us because they're really, really mean, Daddy."

Holding his son on his knee, Le replied with the first reassuring words he could find. "They might have guns, but we have flowers," he said, explaining that the candles and flowers outside the concert hall were there to chase away the dark and protect Brandon while they memorialized the people who died. The little boy then smiled and said, "I feel better."[1]

Today, parents like Angel Le have to help make sense of new, often frightening realities along with the day-to-day challenges families face, creating opportunities and an urgent need for Transformative Resilience. Dinner table conversations now include helping children understand news of issues such as gun violence, divisive politics, poor race relations, and devastating storms.

The world isn't just more unpredictable but our lives are also more complex. Many of today's parents come from the "sandwich generation," juggling careers, caring for both aging parents and young children, and working to maintain their partnerships. Many families are relying—at least in part—on debt or strategic home refinancing to make ends meet. Safety and security are often on the minds of families today.[2]

For a large number of families, wages have stagnated or deteriorated. Many middle-class jobs evaporated during the Great Recession and have never returned. For more and more families, achieving the American Dream feels unattainable. There's an emotional toll of living in these precarious, unequal times.

Families today are also more diverse than ever before. From two-earner households to divorced, single-parent, and blended families, from multiracial families to gay and lesbian households and couples raising adopted children, families are negotiating a number of scenarios that affect their daily routines as well as their identities and how they make sense of the world.

And, just as there is diversity among families, there is diversity within families, particularly with generational divides that can stretch our ability to jointly make meaning of events and come to a collective understanding or align ourselves as families when parents, children, and grandparents can experience turbulence in different ways.

The Type R Family

In many respects our family creates the blueprints for what we believe, who we become, and how we engage with the world. This is cemented in our early years but lasts throughout our lives, carried into our relationships, friendships, careers, and professional and political interactions. As today's families grapple with how to nurture and support solid, lasting relationships to weather the challenges we face and prepare the next generations for a changing world, the ability not only to bounce back but also to spring forward becomes critical.

Much like in organizations, Transformative Resilience in families is a matter of building a shared culture and mindset while negotiating the varying needs and perspectives of those in it. Type R families successfully work through adversity, placing it within a larger context, and together emerge strengthened, more resourceful, and confident.

Type R families also share some characteristics with Type R individuals and must cultivate TR in ways that echo navigating group dynamics in the workplace. These include developing a collective mindset and skills—in the case of families, hopefulness, the ability to forge meaning together, authentic communication, and providing support in ways that lead to growth and greater strength in both adults and children.

While we're in the midst of hardship, disruptive change, or challenges, it's not always easy to be our best selves and embrace the Type R mindset. Under stress, we often revert to dysfunctional childhood behaviors until we recognize that our defense mechanisms have taken over and aren't serving us, our family, or the situation at hand.

We may think that we have to take charge and appear invulnerable when in fact that might be the opposite of what's required.

Or we may plunge into helplessness and depression when that too is ineffective. It's no easy feat, but these are the times when we most need to be aware of unproductive habits and do our best to let down our defenses and share our fears, needs, and concerns with our family members. We need to ask for the support we require to draw on more effective Type R skills.

Although some families are diminished by stressful life and world events, extraordinarily a significant number of others come through strengthened, more confident, and more resourceful. Many experience profound, lasting intimacy, raise well-adjusted children, and nurture Type R individuals.

The research of human development and family experts Nick Stinnett and John DeFrain reinforces the transformative nature of challenges for families. They evaluated information about the home lives of 130 families from a range of socioeconomic statuses, races, ethnic origins, religions, and educational backgrounds to identify the characteristics shared by the strongest of them.

Stinnett and DeFrain found that during a crisis, 75 percent of strong families reported having positive experiences and believed that something good always followed difficult times.[3] On the basis of this finding, the researchers proposed that the strongest households create a sense of positive identity, promote satisfying and fulfilling interaction among members, encourage the development of the family and individual members, and deal with stress. They also found that strong families are created step by step. People in resilient homes have to work at developing TR continually, but the effort provides them with unrivaled support, satisfaction, and meaning.

Type R families encompass the qualities found in the study as well as others. Frequently, when Type R families undergo a stressful life event they emerge with a deepening of their relationships, more effective ways of communicating, newfound confidence in their ability to overcome challenges together, and new skills and abilities. They also emerge with a more profound understanding and appreciation of their loved ones.

The transformation of a relationship through weathering adversity suggests not just a return to a previous way of being but movement through and beyond stress and suffering into a new level of connection. The Type R approach to family is based on cultivating a shared belief that we survive and prosper most through our significant bonds to each other.

What distinguishes Type R families isn't their lack of problems to face or suffering to experience but rather their ability to cope with challenge and changes. They possess the capacity to manage both daily stresses and difficult life crises creatively and effectively. Type R households often anticipate how to prevent trouble before it happens and how to work together to meet inevitable challenges when they occur.

Family Hopefulness

When Suzanna Dennis and Maurice Nsabimana met in graduate school in 2003, they couldn't have known that they'd found in one another a partner whose drastically different, but equally challenging, life experiences would be their greatest asset when they started a family. Maurice, a tall, soft-spoken man, grew up in Rwanda but was studying in Austria in 1994 when his father, a high-ranking government official, was assassinated in an incident that ignited the Rwandan genocide. Suddenly, at age twenty-two, Maurice became the head of the family, and his whole country was plunged into conflict.

At nineteen, Suzanna, a cheerful and take-charge Californian, was seriously injured during a sexual assault while living overseas. A few months later, Suzanna's step-sister and nephew were murdered in what remains an unsolved case. Through these horrific life-changing events, Maurice and Suzanna each learned to reframe their experiences, draw on their reserves of optimism, and practice their ability to use adversity to their advantage.

The Type R skills that each of them had cultivated in themselves became the foundation that steadied them once they had their children, Sofia and Alex, and wrestled with the day-to-day challenges of raising children, maintaining demanding careers, and providing support to their parents and extended family.

One day when Alex was two years old, he was taken to the doctor for a lingering cough. Shockingly, they discovered that he had liver cancer. "When we first received the diagnosis I was afraid my son was going to die," Suzanna explains to us when we speak.[4]

After a couple harrowing weeks, they received good news. Alex's cancer had been detected early and as a result the surgeons could remove the cancerous portion of his liver, allowing the organ to continue to function. "Having survived what I had and also knowing what Maurice had been through, we knew we were going to make it through this, too," says Suzanna, reflecting on her faith and optimism in this extremely difficult time.

One of the most important ways that the two were able to cope was by keeping their challenges in perspective and remaining hopeful. "I used to comfort myself in knowing that we were relatively lucky [and that] there was always someone worse off than we were," says Suzanna. "On one hand, we were very unlucky that he had to go through what he did. On the other hand, we were lucky to catch it early and [with] how well Alex responded to the treatment and having him be cancer free for two years now."

Despite the intense period of crisis they went through, Suzanna and Maurice share the belief that it crystallized a deeper appreciation of their family bonds, a stronger sense of purpose in life, and a dedication to live their values more fully. Out of the crucible of adversity the ordeal has allowed them to be more than what they might have been had they not undergone the experience.

In the uncertainty and pain wrought by a stressful life event, we're reminded of our core values. It's often the case that we aren't aware of the Type R qualities and skills that we as individuals or as families possess until we're tested. There is a wide spectrum in how people cope with adversity, ranging from those who fully embrace Transformative Resilience to those who become mired in old, unproductive habits. However, it's always possible to build on our skills and learn new, more effective ways of coping. Type R individuals and families frequently emerge from stressful life events with a heightened sense of purpose in their lives as well as increased compassion for the struggles of others. Just as with individuals, when families approach challenges with confidence and hope, they are likely to do better and transform difficult experiences into important lessons.[5]

By *hopefulness* we don't mean an attitude of being overly optimistic and looking on the bright side without recognizing difficult circumstances and expressing fears. Rather, hopefulness is the belief that there is a possibility for a better future.

Transformative Resilience is fueled by steadfast shared confidence: we know we'll make it through. If there's a solution to be found, we'll find it; otherwise, we'll find a way to accept things as they are. This belief and the persistent search for solutions increase hope and make family members dynamic participants in coping and adapting. In our darkest hour hope and optimism are essential.

The word *hope* originated in Old English and has a similar meaning in numerous languages: "to leap with expectation." Philosopher Jonathan Lear introduced the notion of radical hope. "What makes this hope radical," Lear wrote, "is that it is directed toward a future goodness that transcends the current ability to understand what it is." Radical hope is not something that already exists but something we work to cultivate and practice. It's our best defense against despair even when despair seems like the most reasonable response. Maintaining hope when confronted with overwhelming circumstances enables us to continue our best efforts.

As we said in Chapter 3, hope is essential to Transformative Resilience. It provides the energy and motivation to overcome adversity. Hope enables a forward-thinking attitude and a Type R mindset—no matter how devastating and overwhelming our current situation, a better future can be imagined.

Catherine Panter-Brick, a professor in the Department of Anthropology at Yale, spent several years living and working in Afghanistan studying the effect of war on resilience and humanitarian policy and public health. She discovered that despite significant exposure to war, individuals and families find ways to adapt and prosper even in the face of significant risk. One characteristic that most stood out to her while watching Afghan families up close was that their hardiness or strength, if described by a single word, was hope.

More than anything these families appeared to focus on getting up each day and securing the resources for a better future rather than on dwelling on the turmoil and traumas of the past. Hope has given meaning and order to these families amid what could otherwise feel like senseless suffering.

Relational Endurance

Pioneering family therapist Virginia Satir proposed that parents are the architects of the family—they set the tone, particularly when children are young. They create the scaffolding and infrastructure that they build on together as a family, including the characteristics and tools that they draw on to make it through challenges.

Parents model these behaviors for their children. Children learn how to communicate by observing their parents' actions, lessons that they carry into adulthood, whether modeling that behavior or reacting to it. Depending on how they choose to cope, parents can be conduits for stress and anxiety or they can create a TR ripple effect within the family.

The emotional well-being of children is affected by the emotional climate between their parents.[6] Transformative Resilience in adults affects not only their own long-term outcomes but also those of their children and other family members. And, Type R parents who respond effectively to adverse circumstances make it easier for their partners to weather challenges and in so doing reduce the negative consequences for their children.

A crisis can be a wake-up call, directing our attention to what truly matters in our lives. Challenging circumstances and mounting pressures provide a couple with opportunities to learn about untapped potential in their relationship, to strengthen their bond, to deepen their commitment, and to build greater trust and closeness as they learn to rely on each other.

When couples cultivate relational endurance, they fortify their relationship against stress and challenges and create the atmosphere for the rest of the family. There's little doubt that when we are confronted with a crisis as a family we become strained, often to the limit. These situations call for us to rally our collective strength to support one another, solve problems, and maintain a sense of integrity and purpose. Confidence in one another—a belief that each of us will do our best for the family—creates the basis for growth. In uniting, we strengthen our capacity to overcome challenges.

During their son Alex's treatment, Suzanna and Maurice both concentrated on the kids, understandably. "The focus was, 'Let's get us through this,'" recalls Maurice. "The balance in our relationship was thrown off during that period because there was just so much we had to do for our kids."

For a time, they treated one another more as business partners than as spouses. Suzanna and Maurice ran through checklists of what needed to be done and what needed to be managed.

Though their relationship suffered for a time, seeing the extent to which they could rely on one another, they came out of the crisis with a greater sense of trust and a deeper appreciation for each other and for their family.

"Being able to count on him and learn to expect so much of Maurice was incredible," Suzanna explains. "He has been such an amazing father and an amazing partner through this, even though we didn't have time to focus on each other while Alex was in the hospital. My love for Maurice grew having seen how he handled everything so well," Suzanna continues. Even though Maurice was working full time, he never missed a single one of Alex's numerous appointments. And he even shaved his head and eyebrows when Alex lost his hair from the chemo. "This is what every father and husband should be," says Suzanna.

And still, despite having one another, it has been difficult for Suzanna and Maurice to return to the challenges of day-to-day life after the emergency was over. The year following Alex's illness was actually the hardest for Suzanna and put even more of a strain on her relationship with Maurice as she grappled with residual feelings from the stressful events. She found herself becoming frustrated, short-tempered, and tearful without knowing why. And, at the same time, she was under the additional pressure of supporting another family member whose relationship was in crisis.

For Maurice, the main stress was adjusting to a regular schedule and mounting demands at work. For months leading up to Alex's illness, it was unclear whether Maurice would continue to have a job. His contract at the World Bank as a data analyst was renewed just as Alex was diagnosed with cancer and Maurice's colleagues were very supportive throughout his treatment. However, Maurice was under significant pressure to rapidly immerse himself in work again after Alex's illness, especially because the World Bank had begun a major restructuring process.

The fifty to sixty hours a week that he now works means he gets home at seven thirty or eight at night, frequently leaving

Suzanna to cook dinner and put the kids to bed. When he walks in, Suzanna is sometimes upset because she misses having him around at dinnertime. But the challenging circumstances they have faced as a couple and a family have ultimately created space for change.

They have begun deliberately putting time aside for one another. Suzanna teases Maurice that she will also begin calling him daily at five thirty to sound the alarm bells that it's time to come home. And Suzanna is in therapy to help her cope with the residual feelings from her son's illness and other past traumas. This is making a significant difference for Suzanna, helping reduce her stress and frustration and giving her a deeper appreciation for her family, the stability Maurice provides, and their willingness to continue to grow together as a couple.

A challenging situation can provide a rare opportunity for us as family members to review, reassess, and refocus our lives. Adversity may also bring a surprising acknowledgment of the importance of relationships that had otherwise been taken for granted. It all has to do with the lens through which we view the challenges that we face, the meaning that we draw from them, the course of action that we choose, and the kind of support that we receive.

Forging Meaning from Adversity

There's nothing like a major disruption in our lives to make us want to understand more fully what's happening, how it came to pass, the future consequences, and what steps we as a family can take to adjust and adapt. For many Type R families, it's a matter of making the challenging situation more understandable, manageable, and meaningful.

Like other groups, families are a patchwork of different perspectives and needs, particularly depending on the age and stage of development of grandparents, parents, and children, that influence how a family makes meaning together. As children get older and form their own opinions, the process of making sense of the world and navigating differing views can also prove to be a challenge.

For this reason Type R families focus on the opportunity to weave the threads of each individual family member's experiences into a cohesive whole so that they feel that life and the world around them do indeed make sense, despite chaos, stress, worry, or despair.

Almost any one of us who struggles with change or who has experienced hardship has raised the question, at least internally, Why? Why did this have to happen to me, to my child, to my parent, or to my family? What did we do to deserve this? Together, families grapple with these kinds of questions while trying to make sense of a changing world.

We may not always find the answers, but the ability to forge meaning together out of adversity provides us with some degree of optimism and the belief in a future beyond the current challenge. How families make sense of a stressful life event and give it meaning plays a major role in their ability to successfully cope and cultivate TR.[7]

Disruptive change, mounting pressures, and major stressful life events, particularly those that have long-lasting impacts, interrupt family culture, structure, and routines, forcing us to adapt and change. The changes that follow are closely tied to the meaning that a family draws from stressful events. Perhaps even more important is the fact that the meaning we find reverberates beyond the immediate circumstances and alters our view of our family itself and the larger world.

We're struck by how some people who face major stressful life events seem to draw strength from these situations. Popular thinking along with research suggests that much of this has to do with finding meaning—as if meaning is out there, a truth waiting to be discovered. It is up to us to forge meaning in challenging times, drawing lessons from adversity, and to deepen our connections and grow.

Authentic Communication

Communication is the foundation of making meaning and ultimately cultivating TR as a family. Yet, in the words of playwright George Bernard Shaw, "The single biggest problem in communication is the illusion that it has taken place." Too often family members convey messages to one another—particularly ones that contain an element of displeasure or anger—that rarely resolve the situation and that often lead to hurt feelings on all sides.

Families have at least two basic styles of communication: affirming, communication that conveys support and caring and encourages a calming influence; and confrontational, yelling, blaming, generalizing that tends to enflame a stressful situation. In fact, all families communicate in both ways, but challenges and stressful life events often make us more confrontational with one another, weakening our family's ability to effectively cope and adapt. It's for this reason that Type R families make significant efforts to emphasize affirming communication to foster growth and development.

When Steve and Caroline Mason's daughter Amanda entered rehab for substance abuse at age nineteen, they learned firsthand how important it was to share their feelings with one another. For many weeks they didn't know whether she would recover. At first, Steve was quiet and reserved, keeping his feelings to himself. But as time went on, he realized that concealing his emotions only amplified his fear and anxiety and sent the wrong message to Caroline. Once he opened up and began discussing how he felt with her, it brought the two of them closer and enabled them to face what the future held for their family, together.

Honest communication is the fundamental tool for beginning to see ourselves and our families in a new light and adapting to changing realities. As Steve and Caroline discovered, they needed to be able to understand each family member's experience and concerns and work together rather than against one another in the face of Amanda's substance use and the many ways her rehabilitation would change the family.

Although Amanda successfully recovered and went on to apply to college, the challenges the family faced around her addiction forced everyone to reflect on who they are individually and how they interact as a family. Their honest communication brought clarity to their difficult situation, encouraged open emotional expression, and promoted collaborative problem solving.

Rather than putting on a façade of invulnerability, Type R family members feel safe to share our fears, doubts, sadness, and concerns. We also focus on authentic and consistent communication and using difficult times as opportunities to transform how we may have previously interacted.

Part of this is a matter of ensuring that our verbal and nonverbal messages are consistent—in other words, we say what we mean and mean what we say—and in this way we avoid sending vague, confusing, or mixed messages to each other. It's communication with emotional integrity.

Often family members develop different understandings of events and their consequences based on snippets of information or gossip. We may even try to make sense of the situation by inserting our greatest wishes or fears. Our experience becomes more understandable and manageable when information and insights are shared and when the meanings of a situation and its repercussions for the family are discussed openly and honestly.

Frequently, when we as parents are concerned or upset we try to shield children from worry by acting as if everything's "normal." Yet, this rarely works. Children sense the underlying anxiety.

On June 24, 2016, Kate Dyson, founder of the *Motherload* blog, woke up as usual to make breakfast for husband, Matt, a radio presenter, and their two daughters, Beth, almost five, and Maggie, two and a half. But Kate soon discovered this wasn't like any other morning.

The day before, UK citizens had gone to the polls to vote on whether the country would leave the European Union, of which it had been a member for over forty years, allowing free movement of people between countries and shaping everything from the country's culture to its economy and laws. The majority of people didn't believe that it would happen, despite rising economic inequality accompanied by growing nationalist and anti-immigrant sentiments in segments of the United Kingdom.

Countless people were in shock, including those who did and those who didn't vote in favor of the referendum, and the country was quickly thrown into uncertainty as to what would happen. The nation's currency plummeted, and hate crimes rose 57 percent in the following days alone, according to the National Police.

As Kate stood stunned in the kitchen, listening to the morning news and trying to pack school lunches, she had to consider how to talk to her children. "What is it, Mama? What's wrong?" asked a precocious Beth. Kate wasn't sure how to explain this potentially life-altering situation to her four-year-old. "As parents when we have children we all think, 'I hope for you that you grow up in a safe and [tolerant] place,'" Kate says, explaining a large part of her upset to us.[8]

In the following days, while Beth played she would suddenly ask Kate, "What is the EU? Why have we left the EU?" Obviously, the issue remained a concern for her. What proved to be a bigger immediate challenge was how to address the increase in racism and attacks on immigrants.[9] Beth asked, "Why are people hurting other people?" Kate and Matt struggled with how to help their older daughter understand. "That's such a complex thing to explain to a four-year-old. In a way it was almost a chip at her innocence—[the idea] that people hurt each other," Kate says.

This situation led Beth to grapple with the issues in a very personal way, worrying for Chinese friends in her preschool class.

"Do they have to go home now?" she asked. Kate explained that the United Kingdom was their home despite some people expressing anti-immigrant sentiments.

Like many parents, Kate and Matt believe that they should protect their children, while being open and explaining issues in an age-appropriate manner. It's critical that kids, even young children, can talk and hear more adult topics in a family context. It's in part what leads to Transformative Resilience in families.

As they contended with the change around them, Beth and Matt instinctively returned to having dinners together. The dinner table became an important place for the family to talk about issues both large and small and for the kids to be a part of conversation about important topics, even if merely by being present.

That ritual helped create a sense of continuity, containment, and safety for Beth and her little sister Maggie as the older girl, in particular, tried to make sense of the uncertainty around her. It helped to create a sense of "it's okay in my home," a feeling that children need in general but that becomes even more critical during times of stress and change.

Children must learn to understand that uncertainty and occasional failures are a part of life and that they, their family, and, where appropriate, their community and country have the resources to meet the challenge. Part of this understanding comes from parents providing concrete examples of how others have successfully risen to challenges and the positive elements in difficult or disruptive events.

Genuinely listening to our children is so important when a family is experiencing a hardship. Yet this can be challenging in our digital age given that technology has also become a major distraction. It's especially significant during difficult periods, when we may feel a stronger urge to pull out our phone and get lost in social media to avoid the situation and one another. Although using technology as an escape is understandable, even healthy to a limited degree, we must monitor how it is affecting our children and how they may be using their devices for avoidance as well. That said, more often than not, one person among us, whether an adult or child, will usually prod and poke and provoke the family out of avoidance and force dialogue.

In particular, when children's emotions and needs are ignored or go unaddressed, they can explode in physical or behavioral signs of suffering. Children sometimes don't know how to communicate their distress. Their first line of defense is often acting out, especially if they are not given another outlet for the emotions they are grappling with. Children need an empathic listener when they are upset.

Sherry Turkle, professor of social studies of science and technology at MIT, notes, "Through the conversational attention of parents, children acquire a sense of enduring connectedness and a habit of talking about their feelings, rather than simply acting on them."[10] When we listen and acknowledge their feelings appropriately, they are able to move through their confusion. If family members provide an outlet for one another to express feelings and attempt to more fully understand the situation, we're able to cope effectively.

But we also have to take into account the diverse needs of those in the family. This means being aware of the different ways in which a situation will affect family members of different ages and how it will affect how they choose to communicate. For example, the EU vote spoke to young and old in very different ways in terms of national versus global identity and in terms of future work prospects for the young versus national health care and retirement for older people. One young woman wrote a moving letter to her family trying to heal the rifts that their differing views had created. "My character and opinions were formed by you.... You taught me to live in the wider world, to really see and value other cultures," she wrote to her parents. "I cannot understand how you could have voted for Britain to leave the EU. I am at a complete loss. This has thoroughly shaken me, my understanding of my family and the country I grew up in."[11]

And as we've seen throughout the chapter, families with young children function differently from how families function when children become adolescents and young adults. Parents' demands for open communication may be viewed by adolescents as prying and intrusive. Adolescent children and their parents must therefore renegotiate patterns of closeness, allowing for increasing separateness, independence, and autonomy. While younger children may need undivided attention and care, older children and teens may prefer to discuss a challenging situation while doing something else to shift focus off of them and make things feel less intense or intimidating.

Whether including a child, teen, or young adult, when problems are identified, it's important to involve family members, including extended family where appropriate, in brainstorming solutions, where each person feels that their thoughts, feelings, and ideas are heard, appreciated, and respected. In Type R families, parents act as directors and coaches, eliciting others' ideas, voicing their own, and encouraging choices wherever possible. Family members speak up, and the contributions of all members, from eldest to youngest, are respected.

Type R families accept and encourage a wide range of emotional expression by adults and children. We assume responsibility for our own feelings and accept others who have feelings different from ours. We value positive exchanges and appreciate humor, even as we cope with difficult circumstances.

We All Need Somebody to Lean On

Pulling together is one of the most important elements in weathering difficulties. Supportive, caring relationships are lifelines for

Transformative Resilience. On one hand, parents play a critical role in providing structure and guiding the family. On the other, extended family and social networks, such as church and support groups, colleagues, acquaintances, and friends, contribute emotional support and advice, information, external resources, and practical help when families face change and difficult times. They also provide a safety net and a sense of security and solidarity. And for some people who don't have the support of or are alienated from family, these communities become a default family.

Parents and families in general need support from a larger community to withstand life's ups and downs. It's not the size of the social network or the regularity of interactions that makes a difference but the authenticity and helpfulness of those in it that counts. Some people are better at offering practical help, others emotional support, but they can all contribute to relieving some of the burden a family may be experiencing when facing disruptive change. Connections to extended family, close friends, and social networks are essential for TR in times of disruption, stress, and strain.

For Maurice and Suzanna, both family and an extended network of friends made all the difference. Maurice's mother came to stay in the first weeks of Alex's illness, and a childhood friend of Suzanna's set up an online page to engage and update their broader community and ask for their support. Sofia's teacher started giving her special attention, extra time and hugs to help her adjust. The family also used the hospital and social services like art therapy and child life specialists for both children.

For Kate and Matt and their kids, the fact that they were able to spend a long weekend with their extended family following the EU vote meant that they were all able to offer support to one another. Together, they grappled with the issues and tried to understand and cope with what it would mean for the entire family and the different generations, from the grandparents to the preteen cousins to Kate and Matt and their young children.

Hope for the Future

As we live with increasing uncertainty, it's more important than ever to cultivate our Type R skills as a family and create networks for ourselves to provide an anchor that grounds us in what's most important. This requires that we care for and nurture our significant relationships so that they can act as a shelter against the storms of twenty-first-century life. We must invest in our relationships with as much care and understanding as we can muster, especially during difficult times.

The reality is that parents and adult family members are juggling a number of different kinds of pressures, from the personal to the professional to the global. Our children are being forced to learn the difficult truths of life far more rapidly than we might like, in part because of the economic and social realities in many parts of the world. This adds a layer of complexity to the challenges that we face on a daily basis and asks us to make our families a safe haven to which we can retreat to find solace, support, and comfort.

The Type R family is far from problem free; however, we apply a mindset in which we forge meaning from our difficult experiences and extract the lessons that can help build confidence, strengthen intimacy, and foster greater trust in one another. As Type R families, we integrate what we've learned into our efforts to live better lives, with the hope that others can benefit from our experience.

As we chart a path through personal, professional, and global challenges, often we turn to our families first in times of change and stress. They help us learn to communicate our needs, hopes, and fears and build skills that we carry throughout our lives. For this reason, families that cultivate Transformative Resilience provide critical foundations and skills for not just surviving in today's world but also thriving.

That's not to say that families can't also be the source of pain and turbulence, even Type R families. This is particularly true when we fall out of sync with loved ones or when our families don't have the skills or resources to meet our needs.

Regardless, Type R families shape how we view and engage with the world in meaningful and lasting ways. By modeling authentic communication, healthy behavior, and continual learning and growth, Type R families build the foundations for putting Transformative Resilience into practice in the various arenas of our lives.

CHAPTER 9

Type R in Action

The best way to predict the future is to invent it.

Alan Hay

WE NOW HAVE the foundations for understanding the power of Transformative Resilience to change us at the individual, professional, local, and global levels. And we're aware of the ripple effect that building our skills can have as Type Rs. A large part of this and the ability to turn challenges into opportunities is actively engaging.

Sometimes when we find ourselves facing challenges or daunting change, having hope alone is a radical act. But that hope also becomes the foundation for our ability to make plans, reinvent our future, and take steps toward it.

Think back to the umbrella of Type R characteristics. How do we begin to harness the winds of change and the storm clouds like Mary Poppins did to take us to new places rife with opportunity? How do we emulate the many inspiring people and organizations that we have met throughout this book, from individuals like Stephanie Decker to business men like Frederick Hutson, from leaders like Joanna Kerr to organizations like EY and the families of Maurice and Suzanna and Matt and Beth?

It's up to each one of us to decide which actions are most appropriate for our lives, careers, organizations, families, and communities at a given time. That said, here are some initial suggestions for actions that we can each take to foster Transformative Resilience and the Type R mindset and skills. These can become catalysts for larger change and can be built on over time.

There are, however, many circumstances in which we can't go it alone and we may first need to address some basics before undergoing a TR Journey. More specifically, although some of these concepts may be helpful across a range of situations, while not impossible, it's difficult to build Transformative Resilience in circumstances in which our basic needs for food, safety, and shelter are not being met.

And there are situations in which individuals, leaders, businesses, families, and even whole communities may need immediate professional support, such as emergency or medical services, psychological and trauma support, and urgent business and technical services to stabilize a situation and lay the groundwork for moving on to a long-term approach for cultivating Transformative Resilience.

With that in mind, this is by no means a comprehensive how-to approach. However, we hope to provide a few thought-provoking ideas to get you started.

Actions for Individuals

Question your default mindset. Examining our attitude is the first step in understanding our response to events and circumstances in our lives, our work, and the world around us. But, the ability to identify our mindset takes time to develop. It helps to start by looking back to train our mental muscles for "mindset alertness"—becoming aware of how our current point of view operates in our lives.

For example, briefly describe a recent stressful life event. What messages do you hear on a regular basis about how you should think about stressful life events and adversity? What do you think about yourself and your ability to face these circumstances? Do you believe that these circumstances are an impediment or an opportunity? As we improve our ability to look backward, we learn to carry those skills forward into the present and more regularly draw on them.

Practice emotional hygiene. Although a certain amount of sadness or frustration are natural, even healthy, after a loss, failure, or stressful life event it's essential that we don't allow them to ultimately overwhelm us and run the show.

One of the keys to doing so is to interrupt recurring cycles of negative inner dialogue. Creating a break gives us a moment for space and reflection that then allows us to choose a new direction. For some, this pause is simply a momentary awareness that we're caught in repetitive thinking and willing ourselves to redirect. But for many of us, especially as we build our skills, it's a process of disrupting habitual thinking repeatedly, including stopping and focusing on our breath rather than on our thoughts, changing our physical environment to help create distance from our initial mental space, or having a conversation with someone we trust to get a fresh perspective.

Connect to the context. It's a fine yet important balance between taking responsibility for ourselves and our lives while also acknowledging the larger context and not blaming ourselves for things outside of our control.

As we've shown throughout the book, large public events and global trends become personal very quickly. And yet many of us face stresses such as layoffs, injuries, illnesses, and failures as personal challenges, thinking "Life happens" or "Why me?" without seeing that many others are experiencing similar situations. We can seek information about the context for what each of us is experiencing to find support, allies, and resources that might help us learn, grow, and respond in productive ways. It's also helpful to elicit feedback from other people who may offer a different, broader perspective so we can see the larger context. We should also give ourselves a break—it's likely not about us.

Examine your relationship to control. When life feels overwhelming, we often lose sight of what we can change, either feeling stymied by the notion that we can't have an impact or feeling overburdened by taking on responsibility for circumstances and factors that are beyond our reach. For this reason, being able to separate out what we can and cannot control can be empowering.

We can start by acknowledging that how we choose to interpret or frame circumstances is within our control as is the response that we choose. As we turn our attention outward, we can ask, How much proximity do I have to the root causes of or decision makers in these circumstances? Do I have skills, information, resources, or relationships that enable me to change or influence this situation? At the same time there are things that may always be outside of our control, whether it's other people, Mother Nature, or just plain bad timing. By identifying what's outside of our control, we can then ask ourselves, If I can't control this circumstance, where can I redirect my energy that might allow me to make more positive changes? Sometimes it's helpful to write down the answers to these questions, making lists or graphs that distinguish between where we can exert our influence and where we have no control.

Clarify what matters. During challenging times, it's important to clarify our values so that they can serve as an anchor as well as help contextualize and buffer us from some of the challenges that we face. This also allows us to identify our priorities and make adjustments to invest our time and energy in those activities that speak to our core beliefs and that are most productive as we move forward.

It helps to step back and ask how we define our lives—is it by relationships with people or by achievement or by having certain experiences? We can then ask, Are these priorities reflected in where I devote my time and energy in coping with this challenging situation? If not, what adjustments do I need to make so that I'm in greater alignment with my beliefs?

Ask different questions. By cultivating inquisitive thinking, we can approach challenges more objectively by asking nonjudgmental questions such as, What's most important now? Or: How can I use this challenge? We are also inquisitive when we imagine the questions someone who has an entirely different view would ask to help expand our thinking and our understanding of the circumstances that we face: How would I see this if I were *X person* whom I respect? This type of questioning is important both in our personal as well as our professional lives. It can also be the jumping off point for collaboration and seeking resources, perspectives, and information that we don't currently have.

Concentrate on learning. With every challenge comes a lesson. We can choose to see challenging circumstances as learning opportunities rather than as a time to shut down. This will make a tremendous difference in our level of Transformative Resilience.

Pain without purpose frequently results in a feeling of helplessness. When we shift our attention from Why me? to What can

I learn from this? we change the challenge from a random act of bad luck to something that we can engage with and shape to our advantage. Some of that learning entails realizing what information, resources, or skills we do and don't have so that we can seek them out either on our own or with the help of others.

We can start by analyzing the situation and jotting down three possible ways in which we might be able to learn something new, including learning related to identifying or managing emotions; learning new interpersonal, technical, or intellectual skills; or gaining new insight in these arenas. The possibilities are ultimately up to each of us. Once we've done this, we are more likely to actively draw lessons from the challenges and struggles and seek out new information or resources as we reflect upon them and choose our strategies for coping, reframing, and acting in the coming weeks, months, and years. And in the end we may be surprised by what we learned when we look back as opposed to what we thought we could or couldn't gain from the experience.

Create a failure CV. The ways in which we consider and respond to mistakes and failures are an essential part of a Type R mindset. Many of us bury our failures and try to hide them from others, if not forget them ourselves. Yet, failure and the ability to learn and build on it is something to be celebrated rather than hidden because of the skills, experience, and growth it can provide.

Reflecting on the value of failure in her work, Melanie Stefan, a scientist at the University of Edinburgh, suggests we create a curriculum vitae of failures. We have to be able to view failures for what they are: do-overs—second chances. Impetus to think and act differently—opportunities to learn and grow. Each of us can make a list of our greatest failures. Write down what was painful about them. Then write down whether those failures provided opportunities or helped in other circumstances later on.

Actions for Leaders

Walk a mile in another's shoes. Leaders can default to certain mindsets, like many of us, which can blind them to how their employees and those outside the organization see their decisions and responses to different events. Type R leaders can expand their view by seeking to understand and empathize with the experiences of others. We can start by asking a series of questions that reflect on our privileges and power as well as the experiences of others.

Try asking, How does a coming organizational change or change in the external world look from where I sit? Then ask, How does it look from the perspective of those in middle management and in entry-level support roles? Are there shared concerns or impacts? Are there ways in which my role shields me from shocks or added pressures (financial, stress levels, workload, and morale)? How can I bridge the gaps between us and build on the commonality we share?

Model Transformative Resilience. Modeling is one of the most effective ways to teach; failure to model or modeling actions inconsistent with what's being imparted weakens efforts to promote TR within organizations, between organizations, and even between leaders working together. As leaders, we can start by demonstrating vulnerability and inviting dialogue about the experiences that have stretched us most and how we are building our own Type R skills, whether at home or at work. Another way of cultivating TR is departing from the age-old notion that leaders have the answer to all challenges. Type R leaders instead help staff and stakeholders ask the right questions and strategize how to find the information needed, how to continue to learn and leverage the best knowledge and best responses.

Reward colleagues for Type R behavior. Changing our mindsets, habits, and behaviors can be challenging. As social animals, we need encouragement and feedback, especially if we're ahead of the crowd in making those changes. We can acknowledge colleagues for actively reframing difficult circumstances, displaying open and direct communication, and seeking out information that will help them learn new skills.

When colleagues exhibit qualities of the Type R mindset and exemplify Transformative Resilience, we must appreciate, encourage, and reward them. This can be as modest as public praise or as elaborate as a formal reward program at the organizational level that acknowledges such behaviors.

Understand the root causes. We all can better learn to accept the circumstances we are presented with. As leaders, developing an understanding of root causes is also critical for choosing how best to respond and to potentially avoid similar scenarios in the future. Some of the questions that may help identify contributing factors include asking whether our business has been disrupted by something that we have the ability to influence or whether the contributing factors must be accepted and adapted to. For instance, Have my actions or inactions snowballed into a crisis? Are there circumstances in my organization or in the world that are causing turbulence for me and possibly for others by creating structural inequities? Has a lack of communication or a common starting point led to further misunderstanding or crisis? Mapping these out, whether mentally or physically, can help us gain clarity about how to respond.

Take a stand. Leaders face the turbulence of the world by cultivating Transformative Resilience. With the Type R skills and strength that comes from TR, we are better positioned to speak out about the issues that cause turbulence for our employees, our organizations, and society, from unethical business or financial practices to racism, inequality, and environmental challenges. By speaking out, we contribute to tackling future challenges before they become crises. We can ask ourselves, Do I have the necessary information to be able to speak up? What would the leader that I most admire do in this situation? Do I have a moral obligation to speak up? What are the consequences for doing so and does the moral obligation or the long-term benefit outweigh those consequences?

Call upon Type R Vision. The elements of Type R Vision provide a more complete picture of the challenges we face and the opportunities that these might present. With Type R Vision, we can contextualize, reframe, see things from multiple perspectives, and project what circumstances might look like over time.

Leaders can apply Type R Vision to existing practices, such as analysis of strengths, weaknesses, opportunities, and threats (SWOT analyses), and take them one step further by overlaying onto them foresight and the benefits of continual learning. We can ask, Are these factors transformed with time? Have they remained the same? Have each of these factors changed for better or worse? What learning has allowed for progress in the cases where things have improved? Different people within an organization have differing views, as do different external actors, and these may be made clearer if leaders take them separately as opposed to negotiating them in a group process. How do the views of different players converge as well as diverge from one another and how do they change our current outlook?

Empower employees in your organization. Even under highly challenging conditions, if people have a sense of agency and efficacy, they're much less likely to be stressed and negatively affected by disruptive situations. It is particularly helpful if we involve our employees early and often in discussions and decision making. We can empower our employees with access to information and transparency. And we can elicit suggestions and recommendations from key stakeholders in new projects, strategies, and initiatives.

Set aside time and resources for continual learning. Rarely do any of us have time to sit and reflect anymore, let alone set aside time for learning as adults. Yet, these are some of the keys to helping us learn from mistakes, adapt to changing environments and circumstances, and innovate.

We can build in opportunities for learning monthly or quarterly, allocating time as if it was a requirement of our jobs. We can ask questions like, What's most surprising in this situation? What's at the outer limits of what seems possible? What information or input am I ignoring or what do I not yet know? Who has perspectives that might help me have a fuller view of what's taking place? Asking questions opens us to new opportunities and creates a more flexible, Type R mindset and is a key part of cultivating Type R Vision.

Actions for Organizations

Identify your existing collective mindset. It's critical that we begin to investigate the overarching culture and mindset shaping the way that we and our colleagues work. Consider creating a dialogue about how people in the organization respond to failure, challenges, stress, and crisis. Use specific examples to draw out detailed information. It may be helpful to use fictitious scenarios to depersonalize challenging events and conversations. Are there unspoken norms about what should be said or done during these times? Do they reflect a shared mindset and culture that accept or reject these types of challenges? We can consider separating out different types of challenges to see whether stress is acceptable but failure is not, for instance.

Cultivate a Type R culture. After gaining an understanding of the group or the organization's starting point, we can identify the areas that most need attention to shift toward a Type R approach. We can then begin to discuss what Transformative Resilience means for our organization within the context of our work situation. Does our organizational culture embrace the notion that it can grow and improve from challenges? How strong are we as a group in each of the six Type R characteristics? What indicators can we use to show the extent to which we are actively putting those characteristics and skills into practice? Can those be included in our organization's planning and review processes so that together we can track concrete progress in areas such as continual learning, applying foresight, framing failures and hardships as opportunities from growth, and so forth?

Create an open flow of information and communication. Creating structures within our organization that allow for sharing information, concerns, challenges, and differing perspectives across departments and across organizational ranks is particularly important. This goes a long way toward developing engagement and ownership in our teams, which is essential for Transformative Resilience. This includes information about challenges we face as an organization, long-range initiatives, and other plans, which have an impact on staff and the organization.

Build a collective memory bank. It's always important to have a reservoir of memories of times when we and our team coped well with change, hardship, or adversity. This is particularly true if the organization is shifting toward a Type R–oriented mindset and culture. The next time our team faces hardship or difficulty, recall and list on a white board one or more of these experiences, and talk about what it means for the team's ability to recover from current difficulties. This will provide reassurance and build confidence that they can make it through new challenges, changes, and stresses as well.

Facilitate learning. To ensure that learning takes place rather than simply finding someone to blame or rehashing events, an appropriate process must be created. Can a retracing of events and outcomes be done in a way that separates people from actions? This allows actions to be critiqued or applauded without judgment of individuals or teams themselves. Can humor be used? (It may be appropriate in some circumstances and not others.) Begin a process of learning by asking whether the lessons emerging from this event build on or contradict what you thought you knew before. How might it serve the organization in the future?

Align organizational values with changes/responses to crisis. Whether an organization initiates change or has to step up to address change, stress, and turbulence in the larger world, those that do best take the time to evaluate whether and how their internal values and external actions are aligned. If they are not aligned, we have to identify the challenges that this poses and the actions that can be taken to create better alignment.

This might mean asking, What are our core values? How do new government policies reflect or challenge those values? What will they mean for our people? For instance, if valuing human capital is one of the organization's main principles, what action do we need to take to ensure that it is upheld during internal processes of change? What action do we need to take to show that we follow through according to our values when there is an external crisis or policy change? Are we "walking our talk" as an organization and, if not, what is keeping us from doing so? How can doing so contribute to Transformative Resilience in our staff and in our organization?

Don't go it alone. We now know that many Type R organizations and businesses improve their Transformative Resilience while contributing to that of others in the broader community. As Type Rs, we may already know who our key stakeholders are and the ways in which we mutually support one another. But unforeseen circumstances might present us with both unexpected challenges and opportunities to roll up our sleeves and make a contribution to the strength and health of a broader community, whether local or global. In doing so, we may boost the morale of those in our organization, create future synergies, and initiate the TR ripple effect.

Actions for Parents and Families

Cultivate a Type R family culture through stories. Adults and children who know their families through stories of success and failure and who have incorporated new stories over the years fare the best in the midst of disruptive change, stress, and challenging times. It's important that each of us consider how stories play a role in our family. Ask, Have we taken the time to talk through a difficult event together in a way that shapes it into a meaningful story? Parents can try playing "Remember When," a game recalling a particularly difficult time in a child's life that he or she not only endured but overcame and was strengthened by. Recall how grandparents or other relatives overcame challenges and hardships. We can even ask elders to tell their stories to our family themselves.

Invite differing views. Draw a picture to initiate a conversation about what's most concerning to different family members about a given event, how they understand themselves, and how they understand the world they live in. Drawing adds play to the process of identifying fears, grievances, and concerns that the family needs to acknowledge and address. It can also shift dynamics to help get beyond entrenched views in cases where family members have differing needs or differing relationships to events.

Practice listening. For those of us who were raised in homes where emotions were considered taboo and to be avoided at all cost, it's not surprising that feelings still are a mystery to us. Learning to respond empathically to our family members' emotions is critical, especially during challenging times. We can start by letting our spouse or partner or child say whatever they need to in order to express themselves. They can talk about their day, the difficult situation that's occurring in the family, what's been on their mind lately. As the receiver, simply listen to whatever the other person has to say, make eye contact, and give an occasional affirming head nod or "mhm." After a few minutes, change roles so that you have a turn to speak in an uninterrupted stream of consciousness.

Practice and model self-care. Children, especially young children, learn by example. But we all are influenced by one another's behavior in our families—partners, siblings, and grandparents. It's vital to make ourselves a good example, setting aside time to exercise, eat well, spend time with friends, and recharge. In the midst of a challenging time, it's easy to get bogged down in the serious tasks that must be attended to. However, it's important to make sure we and our loved ones have time to have fun and have downtime to relax. Encouraging our loved ones to care for themselves and even have fun helps them better cope with stressful life events.

Maintain a hopeful attitude. In the midst of a difficult or painful situation, one of the most helpful things that we can do is encourage family members to look at the circumstance in a wider context and sustain a long-term point of view. Sadly, we're inclined to notice and remember the negative things that happen during the day. Positive interactions and situations are also plentiful, but we often neglect to notice or remember them.

At the end of each day, ask each family member to name at least a couple of positive things that happened during the day and why they were valuable. This exercise only takes a few minutes, but a hopeful and positive outlook enables family members to see the good things in life and persevere even in the most challenging times.

Gather resources to support your family. Supportive, caring relationships are at the heart of TR. Extended family and social networks provide emotional support and advice, information, external resources, and practical help when families face change and difficult times. Keep in mind that support comes in different shapes and sizes and forms. We can take a moment to make a list of our support network and think through what each person or group excels at or can be counted on for. What each person has to offer is probably different—some people are better at offering hands-on help, others an empathetic ear, but they all contribute to relieving some of the load we carry.

* * *

We all continue to be tested as individuals, members of a family, leaders, entrepreneurs, and citizens of a national and global community. Whether or not the challenges we face shake us to our core, there are always unexpected gifts waiting to be discovered.

Since we began our research for this book, the storms we face personally and collectively have become even more ferocious and visible. We're juggling more and calling on the essential principles of Transformative Resilience for turning challenges into opportunities. And sometimes it doesn't come naturally. Like you, we're continuing to learn. Although none of us may have chosen to experience the challenges we face, in hindsight we're richer, stronger, and wiser for them.

We're also aware that more than ever Type Rs need a strong moral compass. We must acknowledge that as we learn to adapt to, reframe, and redirect our energy away from that which we can't change—it is equally important to speak up on behalf of ourselves and others. Transformative Resilience isn't a matter of being presented with injustices or poor behavior and bending to accommodate it. The world desperately needs a Type R revolution and advocates for change. It is up to us to create the world we want to live in, both near and far and in small and large ways.

Whether you're an aspiring Type R or you're well on your way to being one, we hope you find inspiration, understanding, and guidance from the insights in this book. Change starts with us as individuals—and that's only the beginning. By changing ourselves, we can bring the benefits of Type R to our colleagues, businesses, families, communities, and political and global arenas in which we engage. So the next time you see a friend, a colleague, your boss, a team you're interacting with, or even a whole community grappling with a challenge, keep in mind that they too may be working toward becoming more of a Type R. By modeling this behavior personally and professionally, individually and collectively, we can encourage and support others in their pursuit of Transformative Resilience.

Myths and fairy tales remind us that there is a multitude of ways to overcome adversity and to use it to learn, grow, and evolve. The key to harnessing the power of the storm is to look for the deeper meaning and the transformative opportunity, and then to get the support each of us needs to spring forward.

As we face new and mounting challenges and look for solutions, we welcome hearing from you about what's making you hopeful and what's working. There's nothing like sharing encouragement and inspiration to motivate all of us to stay engaged in our own lives and work and to continue to pursue positive change in the larger world.

Please look for us at
www.type-r-resilience.com

Acknowledgments

No book is written alone. Inevitably, there are a number of people who offer invaluable support and encouragement along the way.

This book would not have been possible without the investments from people like Maurice Nsabimana, Suzanna Dennis, Wendy R. Anderson, Frederick Hutson, Joanna Kerr, Akira Thompson, Jonathan Blake, Jill Warren, Ursula Rakova, and Tracy Mann, who trusted us with their stories and were incredibly generous with their time. We would also like to thank the people who believed in the project and talked to us about their work, including Michelle Settecase, Fleur Bothwick, David Croft, and Chris Ruane. And we would like to thank academics and experts Mark Seery, Tim Vogus, Ellen Langer, and John Gerzema, who openly and enthusiastically shared their wealth of knowledge and years of research.

We would like to extend a huge thank-you to those who over many years have been our mentors, friends, advisers, and champions: Steve Andress, John Harris, David Lenihan, Mark Schoder, Ron Cornell, Darlene Collins, Hilda Lando, and Ralph Colao, for Stephanie. For Ama: Heather Grady, Mary Robinson, Anya

Schiffrin, Joseph Stiglitz, Mila Rosenthal, Ignacio Saiz, Chris Jochnick, Sarah Gammage, and Mark McLane, to name a few.

It goes without saying that this book would not have been possible without the ongoing enthusiasm of our editor Colleen Lawrie, the invaluable input of Jane von Mehren, the support of the PublicAffairs editing, publicity, and marketing teams, and the PR support of the fantastic team at Cave Henricks Communications. We would also be remiss not to acknowledge the support of Toni Poynter in shaping our book proposal. And, we would like to thank the three exceptional young women who provided assistance with background and marketing research at various stages in the project—Kanar Patruss, Zoryana Melesh, and Thembi Mdachi.

We would never have made it this far without our family, adopted family, and trusted advisers. JD Marston, Ama's father, proved to be a huge support and source of inspiration as he himself showed us day by day what the spirit of persistence and adaptability means in the face of life's unexpected challenges. Over many a year Marian Small has supported us in our Transformative Resilience as a sister and aunt, has kept us healthy, and has plied us with her medical and wellness expertise. We also are grateful to count Irene Michon, Emily Michon, and Christopher Martell among our family.

Cathy and Dan Warren and Teresa Matazzoni and Ron Parodi have been there over countless years through thick and thin and provided a California home for several weeks for Ama while we finished the book. Celeste Fremon has continued to provide invaluable support and feedback as a long-time friend and award-winning journalist. Lisa Wilson, Sitara Cave, and Ruth Lathrop, who have become like family, have been a huge support over many years. The Segal family have also been loyal friends and supporters over decades, and Bill Leslie and Denise Gonzales have continually proven themselves to be trusted advisers.

Ama's London friends have been invaluable as have a number of friends who have lent support from afar through the years that have led her to learn about Transformative Resilience and the power of calling on others. These include Nuria Molina, Elisa Peter, Sarah Wykes, Rowena Chapman, Francesca Vinti, Jeneve and Edson Monteschio, Oliva Walker, Katie Hair, Claire Langley, Judy Slater, Youmna Chlala, Ivy Young, the Wallgren-Pope family, the Tethong-Simonian family, Aisha Barbeau, Jeanne Merrill, Khisha Clarke, Bianca Mader, Anishiya Taneja, Alison and Jessica Ritz, Inara George, Helen Verhoeven, and the extended Crossroads School and Columbia University School of International and Public Affairs communities. Ama would also like to thank former colleagues like Kirk Herbertson and Kim Thompson who went the extra mile as well as Peter Chowla, Kit Vaughan, Ines Smyth, Georgia Taylor, and Wise Development, among numerous others, who have offered support through ups and downs. We are lucky to say that there are many more of you—both friends as well as colleagues. Hopefully, you know who you are and know that you are appreciated and counted as part of the success of this book.

And, finally, we would like to show our gratitude to one another for years of support, laughter, tears, grit, and now a book together. It is a rare honor to work on a project as mother and daughter.

Notes

Prologue

1. Scott Hensley and Alyson Hurt, "Stressed Out: Americans Tell Us About Stress in Their Lives," National Public Radio, July 7, 2014.
2. American Psychological Association, "2015 Stress in America," www.apa.org/news/press/releases/stress/2015/snapshot.aspx.

Chapter 1: Meeting the Rising Tides in a Turbulent and Changing World

1. Thin Lei Win, "Intrepid PNG Woman Leads Relocation of Island Community Hit by Climate Change," Thomas Reuters Foundation, August 8, 2014, http://news.trust.org//item/20140807164800-6o7xb/.
2. Stéphanie Thomas, "Globalization for the 99%: Can We Make It Work for All?" World Economic Forum, July 6, 2016, www.weforum.org/agenda/2016/07/globalization-for-the-99-can-we-make-it-work-for-all.
3. David Wessell, "Big U.S. Firms Shift Hiring Abroad," *Wall Street Journal*, April 19, 2011.
4. Internal Displacement Monitoring Centre, *Global Estimates 2015: People Displaced by Disasters* (Geneva: Internal Displacement Monitoring Centre, July 2015).
5. Elliot Smith and Philip Kuntz, "CEO Pay 1,795-to-1 Multiple of Wages Skirts U.S. Law," Bloomberg Business News, April 30, 2013,

www.nationaalregister.nl/sites/www.nationaalregister.nl/files/bestanden/20130430_bloomberg_1795_to_1_multiple_of_wages_skirts_us_law.pdf.

6. Oxfam International, "Wealth: Having It All and Wanting More," www.oxfam.org/en/research/wealth-having-it-all-and-wanting-more.
7. Laura Barcella, "What It's Really Like to Move Back in with Your Parents," Refinery 29, June 23, 2015, www.huffingtonpost.com/refinery29.com/what-its-really-like-to-m_b_7648578.html.
8. Robin McKie, "'We Have Only Four Years Left to Act on Climate Change—America Has to Lead,'" *Guardian*, January 17, 2009.
9. Rick Gladstone, "UNICEF Calls 2014 One of Worst Years for Children," *New York Times*, December 8, 2014.
10. Andrew Zolli, "A Shift to Humility: Resilience and Expanding the Edge of Change," *On Being with Krista Tippett*, National Public Radio, May 15, 2013.
11. Jennifer Medina, "With Dry Taps and Toilets, California Drought Turns Desperate," *New York Times*, October 2, 2014.
12. California Department of Food and Agriculture, "California Agricultural Production Statistics: 2015 Crop Year Report," www.cdfa.ca.gov/statistics/.
13. Chris Burgess, "Students Choose Failure over Uncertainty: Broken Job-Hunting System Has College Seniors Retaking Year," *Japan Times*, April 19, 2011.
14. Pamela Weintraub, "The Dr. Who Drank Infectious Broth, Gave Himself an Ulcer, and Solved a Medical Mystery," *Discovery Magazine*, April 8, 2010.
15. C. M. Cox, *Genetic Studies of Genius: The Early Mental Traits of Three Hundred Geniuses* (Stanford, CA: Stanford University Press, 1926).
16. A. L. Duckworth, C. Peterson, M. D. Matthews, and D. R. Kelly, "Grit: Perseverance and Passion for Long-Term Goals," *Journal of Personality and Social Psychology* 92 , no. 6 (2007): 1087–1101.
17. S. R. Maddi, "Hardiness Training at Illinois Bell Telephone," in *Health Promotion Evaluation*, edited by J. P. Opatz, 101–115 (Stevens Point, WI: National Wellness Institute, 1987).

Chapter 2: Transformative Resilience and the Adversity Sweet Spot

1. Lawrence Smith, "House Committee Approves Bill Backed by Hero of March 2nd Tornado," February 27, 2013, www.wdrb.com

/story/21417156/house-committee-approves-bill-backed-by-stephanie-decker.

2. Stephanie Decker, "Courage in the Storm—Surviving Amputation," TED video, 14:25, June 30, 2014, TEDxChapmanU, www.youtube.com/watch?v=bX8QMO9YvLs.
3. Peter Smith, "Ind. Mom Turned Amputee by Tornado Continues Recovery," *Louisville Courier-Journal,* February 28, 2013, www.usatoday.com/story/news/nation/2013/02/28/indiana-tornado-mom-lost-legs-anniversary/1953107/.
4. Haruki Murakami, *Kafka on the Shore* (New York: Vintage, 2005).
5. Jennifer Baker, Caroline Kelly, Lawrence G. Calhoun, Arnie Cann, and Richard G. Tedeschi, "An Examination of Posttraumatic Growth and Posttraumatic Depreciation: Two Exploratory Studies" *Journal of Loss and Trauma* 13 (2008): 450–465.
6. Richard G. Tedeschi and Lawrence G. Calhoun, *Trauma and Transformation: Growing in the Aftermath of Suffering* (Thousand Oaks, CA: Sage Publications, 1995).
7. M. D. Seery and W. J. Quinton, "Understanding Resilience: From Negative Life Events to Everyday Stressors," *Advances in Experimental Psychology* 54 (2016): 181–245.
8. Mark Seery, interview with authors, July 18, 2016.
9. Gene Weingarten, "Pearls Before Breakfast: Can One of the Nation's Great Musicians Cut through the Fog of a D.C. Rush Hour? Let's Find Out," *Washington Post,* April 8, 2007.
10. Steven M. Southwick et al., "Resilience Definitions, Theory, and Challenges: Interdisciplinary Perspectives," *European Journal of Psychotraumatology* 5 (2014): 25338.
11. Joshua M. Smyth, "Written Emotional Expression: Effect Sizes, Outcome Types and Moderating Variables," *Consulting and Clinical Psychology* 66, no. 1 (1998): 174–184.
12. Hamilton Bean, Lisa Keränen, and Margaret Durfy, "'This Is London': Cosmopolitan Nationalism and the Discourse of Resilience in the Case of the 7/7 Terrorist Attacks," *Rhetoric and Public Affairs* 14, no. 3 (Fall 2011): 427–464.
13. Ed Diener, Eunkook M. Suh, Richard Lucas, and Heidi L. Smith, "Subjective Well-Being: Three Decades of Progress," *Psychological Bulletin* 125 (1999): 276–302.
14. J. Xu and Q. Liao, "Prevalence and Predictors of Posttraumatic Growth Among Adult Survivors One Year Following 2008 Sichuan Earthquake," *Journal of Affective Disorders* 133, nos. 1–2 (2011): 274–280. doi:10.1016/j.jad.2011.03.034.

15. H. Hopp, A. S. Troy, and I. B. Mauss, "The Unconscious Pursuit of Emotion Regulation: Implications for Psychological Health," *Cognitive Emotion* 25, no. 3 (April 2011): 532–545.
16. A. Keller, K. Litzelman, L. E. Wisk, T. Maddox, E. R. Cheng, P. D. Creswell, and W. P. Witt, "Does the Perception that Stress Affects Health Matter? The Association with Health and Mortality," *Health Psychology* 31, no. 5 (September 2012): 677–684.
17. Jeremy P. Jamieson, Wendy Berry Mendes, and Matthew K. Nock, "Improving Acute Stress Responses: Current Directions," *Psychological Science* 22, no. 1 (2013): 51–56.
18. S. E. Taylor et al., "Relation of Oxytocin to Psychological Stress Responses and Hypothalamic-Pituitary-Adrenocortical Axis Activity in Older Women," *Psychosomatic Medicine* 66, no. 2 (2006): 238–245.
19. Kathryn Schulz, *Being Wrong: Adventures in the Margin of Error* (New York: HarperCollins, 2010).
20. Randall E. Stross, *The Wizard of Menlo Park: How Thomas Alva Edison Invented the Modern World* (New York: Broadway Books, 2008).
21. Jason S. Moser, H. S. Schroder, C. Heeter, T. P. Moran, and Y. H. Lee, "Mind Your Errors: Evidence for a Neural Mechanism Linking Growth Mind-Set to Adaptive Posterror Adjustments," *Psychological Science* 22, no. 12 (2011): 1484–1489.
22. D. D. Danner, D. A. Snowdon, and W. V. Friesen, "Positive Emotions in Early Life and Longevity: Findings from the Nun Study," *Journal of Personality and Social Psychology* 80, no. 5 (2001): 804–813.
23. Barbara L. Fredrickson, "Are You Getting Enough Positivity in Your Diet?" *Greater Good Magazine,* June 21, 2011, https://greatergood.berkeley.edu/article/item/are_you_getting_enough_positivity_in_your_diet.
24. Jack J. Bauer and George A. Bonanno, "Doing and Being Well (for the Most Part): Adaptive Patterns of Narrative Self-Evaluation During Bereavement," *Journal of Personality* 69 (June 2001): 3.
25. Barbara L. Fredrickson, Roberta A. Mancuso, Christine Branigan, and Michele M. Tugade, "The Undoing Effect of Positive Emotions," *Motivation and Emotions* 24, no. 4 (2000): 237–258.
26. Barbara L. Fredrickson, "The Role of Positive Emotions in Positive Psychology: The Broaden-and-Build Theory of Positive Emotions," *American Psychologist* 56 (2001): 218–226, at 222.

Chapter 3: Type R: The Mindset for Our Time

1. Jonathan Blake, interview with authors, June 28, 2016.
2. Ellen Langer, *Counterclockwise: Mindful Health and the Power of Possibility* (New York: Ballantine, 2009).
3. Ellen Langer, interview with authors, July 16, 2016.
4. Manny Fernandez, Richard Fausset, and Alan Blinder, "After 1963, a Silence Fell Upon Dallas. Not This Year," *New York Times*, July 15, 2016; Dean Keith Simonton, *Greatness: Who Makes History and Why* (New York: Guilford Press, 1994).
5. Barack Obama, remarks at memorial service for fallen Dallas police officers, The White House Office of the Press Secretary, July 12, 2016.
6. Kenneth Smith, *Émile Durkheim and the Collective Consciousness of Society* (New York: Anthem Press, 2014).
7. Thomas J. Scheff, "Shame and Conformity: The Deference-Emotion System," *American Sociological Review* 53, no. 3 (1988): 395–406.
8. Carol S. Dweck, *Mindsets and Math/Science Achievement* (New York: Carnegie Corporation of New York-Institute for Advanced Study Commission on Mathematics and Science Education, 2008), www.growthmindsetmaths.com/uploads/2/3/7/7/23776169/mindset_and_math_science_achievement_-_nov_2013.pdf.
9. Carol S. Dweck, *Mindset: How You Can Fulfil Your Potential* (New York: Robinson, 2012).
10. Rebecca Solnit, "'Hope Is an Embrace of the Unknown': Rebecca Solnit on Living in Dark Times," *Guardian*, July 15, 2016.
11. C. R. Snyder, "Hope Theory: Rainbows in the Mind," *Psychological Inquiry* 13, no. 4 (2002): 249–275.

Chapter 4: Harnessing the Storm: The Type R Characteristics

1. Akira Thompson, interview with authors, July 12, 2016.
2. R. F. Benus, S. den Daas, J. M. Koolhaas, and G. A. van Oortmerssen, "Routine Formation and Flexibility in Social and Non-Social Behavior of Aggressive and Non-Aggressive Male Mice," *Behaviour* 112 (1990): 176–193.
3. Todd B. Kashdan and Jonathan Rottenberg, "Psychological Flexibility as a Fundamental Aspect of Health," *Clinical Psychology Review* 30 (2010): 467–480.

4. J. B. Rotter, "Generalized Expectancies for Internal versus External Control of Reinforcements," *Psychological Monographs* 80, no. 1 (1966), www.soc.iastate.edu/Sapp/soc512Rotter.pdf.
5. Peter Jaret, "The Surprising Benefits of Stress," *Greater Good Magazine,* October 20, 2015, http://greatergood.berkeley.edu/article/item/the_surprising_benefits_of_stress.
6. Mark Seery, interview with authors, July 18, 2016.
7. S. S. Luthar, "Vulnerability and Resilience: A Study of High Risk Adolescents," *Child Development* 62, no. 3 (1991): 600–616.
8. Wendy R. Anderson, interview with authors, July 23, 2015. Additional interviews were conducted in 2016.
9. Kelly McGonigal, *The Upside of Stress: Why Stress Is Good for You, and How to Get Good At It* (New York: Avery, 2015).
10. Matthias J. Gruber, Bernard D. Gelman, and Charan Ranganath, "States of Curiosity Modulate Hippocampus-Dependent Learning via the Dopaminergic Circuit," *Neuron* 84 (2014): 486–496.
11. Cathie Hammond, "Impacts of Lifelong Learning upon Emotional Resilience, Psychological and Mental Health: Fieldwork Evidence," *Oxford Review of Education* 30 (2004): 551–568.
12. Roy F. Baumeister, Kathleen D. Vohs, Jennifer Aaker, and Emily N. Garbinsky, "Some Key Differences between a Happy Life and a Meaningful Life," *Journal of Positive Psychology* 8, no. 6 (2013): 505–516.
13. Mount Sinai Medical Center, "Have a Sense of Purpose in Life? It May Protect Your Heart," *Science Daily,* March 6, 2015, www.sciencedaily.com/releases/2015/03/150306132538.htm.
14. Adam Grant, *Originals: How Non-conformists Change the World* (New York: WH Allen, 2016).
15. Viktor E. Frankl, *Man's Search for Meaning* (Boston: Beacon Press, 2006).
16. Jill Warren, interview with authors, June 24, 2016. Additional interviews were conducted in 2016.
17. Brooke C. Feeney and Nancy L. Collins, "A New Look at Social Support: A Theoretical Perspective on Thriving through Relationships," *Personality and Social Psychology Review* 19, no. 2 (2015): 113–147.
18. S. Cohen, W. J. Doyle, R. Turner, C. M. Alper, and D. P. Skoner, "Sociability and Susceptibility to the Common Cold," *Psychological Science* 14, no. 5 (2003): 389–395.
19. Julianne Holt-Lunstad, Timothy B. Smith, and J. Bradley Layton, "Social Relationships and Mortality Risk: A Meta-Analytic Review," *PLoS Medicine* 7, no. 7 (2010): e1000316.

20. Yumie Ono, H. C. Lin, K. Y. Tzen, H. H. Chen, P. F. Yang, W. S. Lai, J. H. Chen, M. Onozuka, and C. T. Yen, "Active Coping with Stress Suppresses Glucose Metabolism in the Rat Hypothalamus," *Stress* 12, no. 2 (2012): 207–217.
21. McGonigal, *Upside of Stress.*
22. Dean Keith Simonton, *Greatness: Who Makes History and Why* (New York: Guilford Press, 1994).

CHAPTER 5: TRANSFORMERS: THE TYPE R INDIVIDUAL

1. Sonia Sotomayor, *My Beloved World* (New York: Knopf, 2015).
2. Wendy R. Anderson, interview with authors, July 23, 2015. Additional interviews were conducted in 2016.
3. Charles Duhigg, *The Power of Habit* (New York: Random House, 2012).
4. I. Veith, *Hysteria: The History of a Disease* (Chicago: University of Chicago Press, 1965).
5. A. Smith, *The Theory of Moral Sentiments* (New York: Augustus M. Kelley, 1966). Original work published 1759.
6. Nicholas Christakis, "The Hidden Influence of Social Networks," TED video, 20:59, February 2010, www.ted.com/talks/nicholas_christakis_the_hidden_influence_of_social_networks.
7. James H. Fowler and Nicholas A. Christakis, "Dynamic Spread of Happiness in a Large Social Network: Longitudinal Analysis over 20 Years in the Framingham Heart Study," BMJ 337 (2008): a2338.
8. R. Gray and S. L. Beilock, "Hitting Is Contagious: Experience and Action Induction," *Journal of Experimental Psychology: Applied* 17, no. 1 (2011): 49–59.
9. Noah J. Goldstein, Steve J. Martin, and Robert C. Cialdini, *Yes: 50 Scientifically Proven Ways to Be Persuasive* (New York: Free Press, 2008).
10. Malala Yousafzai, Nobel lecture, Oslo, Norway, December 10, 2014, www.nobelprize.org/nobel_prizes/peace/laureates/2014/yousafzai-lecture_en.html.

CHAPTER 6: NAVIGATING UNCHARTED WATERS: THE TYPE R LEADER

1. Eva Dienel, "A Conversation with PepsiCo Chairman and CEO Indra Nooyi: How Do You Promote Transformation?" *Business and*

Social Responsibility (blog), October 30, 2014, www.bsr.org/our-insights/blog-view/a-conversation-with-pepsico-chairman-and-ceo-indra-nooyi-how-do-you-promote.

2. PepsiCo, *Annual Report 2016,* www.pepsico.com/docs/album/annual-reports/pepsico-inc-2016-annual-report.pdf.
3. Gary Burnison, "How Pepsi's Indra Nooyi Learned to Be a CEO," *Fast Company,* April 29, 2011, www.fastcompany.com/1750645/how-pepsis-indra-nooyi-learned-be-ceo.
4. Michael Usmeen, "America's Best Leaders: Indra Nooyi, PepsiCo CEO," *US News & World Report,* November 19, 2008, www.usnews.com/news/best-leaders/articles/2008/11/19/americas-best-leaders-indra-nooyi-pepsico-ceo.
5. Eben Harrell, "Succession Planning: What the Research Says," *Harvard Business Review,* December 2016, https://hbr.org/2016/12/succession-planning-what-the-research-says.
6. John Gerzema and Michael D'Antonio, *The Athena Doctrine: How Women (and the Men Who Think Like Them) Will Rule the Future* (New York: John Wiley and Sons, 2013).
7. Ronald Heifetz and Marty Linsky, *Leadership on the Line: Staying Alive through the Dangers of Leading* (Boston: Harvard Business School Press, 2002).
8. Albert Schweitzer, *Thoughts for Our Times* (Mount Vernon, NY: Peter Pauper Press, 1975).
9. Nick Petrie, *Vertical Leadership Development—Part 1: Developing Leaders for a Complex World* (white paper, Center for Creative Leadership, 2014), www.ccl.org/wp-content/uploads/2015/04/VerticalLeadersPart1.pdf.
10. Joanna Kerr, interview with authors, July 16, 2015. Additional interviews were conducted in 2015 and 2016.
11. Francesca Gino and Gary P. Pisano, "Why Leaders Don't Learn from Success," *Harvard Business Review,* April 2011, https://hbr.org/2011/04/why-leaders-dont-learn-from-success.
12. *The CEO Report: Embracing the Paradoxes of Leadership and the Power of Doubt* (Oxford: Saïd Business School at University of Oxford and Heidrick & Struggles, 2015), www.sbs.ox.ac.uk/sites/default/files/Press_Office/Docs/The-CEO-Report-Final.pdf.
13. Daniel Kahneman, *Thinking Fast and Slow* (New York: Penguin, 2012).
14. Joanna Kerr, "Greenpeace Apology to Inuit for Impacts of Seal Campaign," Greenpeace, June 25, 2014, www.greenpeace.org/canada/en/blog/Blogentry/greenpeace-to-canadas-aboriginal-peoples-work/blog/53339/.

15. Joshua Ostroff, "'Angry Inuk' Explores the Inuit Fight to Protect the Seal Hunt," *Huffington Post,* November 19, 2016, www.huffingtonpost.ca/2016/11/19/angry-inuk-film_n_12527482.html.
16. Vivek K. Wadhera, "Losing Touch: Power Diminishes Perception and Perspective," Kellogg Insight, Kellogg School of Management, Northwestern University, November 1, 2009, https://insight.kellogg.northwestern.edu/article/losing_touch.
17. Green Peak Partners, "Research Results: Nice Guys Finish First When It Comes to Company Performance," Market Wired, June 15, 2010, www.marketwired.com/press-release/research-results-nice-guys-finish-first-when-it-comes-to-company-performance-1276170.htm.
18. Chris Ruane, interview with authors, November 24, 2016.
19. Shauna Shapiro, "Does Mindfulness Make You More Compassionate?" *Greater Good Magazine,* February 27, 2013, https://greatergood.berkeley.edu/article/item/does_mindfulness_make_you_compassionate.
20. Paul H. O'Neill, interviewed by Robert M. Wachter, "In Conversation with . . . Paul H. O'Neill, MPA," Patient Safety Network, January 2017, https://psnet.ahrq.gov/perspectives/perspective/213/in-conversation-with--paul-h-oneill-mpa.
21. Martha Lagace, "Paul O'Neill: Values into Action," HBS Working Knowledge, November 4, 2002, http://hbswk.hbs.edu/archive/3159.html.
22. Charles Duhigg, *The Power of Habit* (New York: Random House, 2013).
23. Robert Safian, "It's Got to Be a Passion, It's Got to Be Your Calling: Indra Nooyi," *Fast Company,* October 14, 2014.
24. Kotter International, "Think You're Communicating Enough? Think Again," *Forbes,* June 14, 2011.
25. Reinhardt Krause, "Alcoa's Paul O'Neill Relied on Analysis and Safety to Boost His Company to the Forefront," *Investor's Business Daily,* May 21, 2001.
26. Frederick Hutson, interview with authors, June 11, 2015. Additional interviews were conducted in 2016 and 2017.
27. Jim Collins and Morten T. Hansen, "Great by Choice: How to Manage through Chaos," *Fortune,* October 2011, www.jimcollins.com/article_topics/articles/how-to-manage-through-chaos.html#articletop.
28. Kurt April, Babar Dharani, and Kai Peters, "Leader Career Success and Locus of Control Expectancy," *Academy of Taiwan Business Management Review,* 2011, www.ashridge.org.uk/Media-Library

/Ashridge/PDFs/Publications/LeaderCareerSuccess&LocusOfControlExpectancy.pdf.

Chapter 7: We're All in It Together: The Type R Organization

1. "1. Massimo Bottura," *Chef's Table*, season 1, episode 1, directed by David Gelb (Netflix, April 2015).
2. "Global Human Capital Trends 2014: Engaging the 21st-Century Workforce," Deloitte, www2.deloitte.com/global/en/pages/human-capital/articles/human-capital-trends-2014.html.
3. Sigal Barsade, "The Ripple Effect: Emotional Contagion and Its Influence on Group Behaviour," *Administrative Science Quarterly* 47, no. 4 (2002): 644–675.
4. Michelle Settecase, interview with authors, January 23, 2017.
5. EY, "Flexibility Makes It All Possible," www.ey.com/us/en/about-us/our-people-and-culture/diversity-and-inclusiveness/ey-infographic-flexibility-makes-it-all-possible.
6. Fleur Bothwick (EMEIA Director of Diversity and Inclusion at EY), personal communication, June 29, 2017.
7. Lou Carlozo, "Ernst & Young Steps Up for Same-Sex Partners," Reuters, January 20, 2012.
8. "Retired U.S. General Stanley McChrystal Talks Leadership Strategy," MIT Management Sloan School, February 18, 2015, http://mitsloan.mit.edu/newsroom/articles/retired-u-s-general-stanley-mcchrystal-talks-leadership-strategy/.
9. Martin Dewhurst, Matthew Guthridge, and Elizabeth Mohr, "Motivating People: Getting beyond Money," McKinsey & Company, November 2009, www.mckinsey.com/business-functions/organization/our-insights/motivating-people-getting-beyond-money.
10. Irving L. Janis, *Victims of Groupthink* (New York: Houghton Mifflin, 1972).
11. Deloitte, *The 2016 Deloitte Millennial Survey: Winning Over the Next Generation of Leaders* (Japan: Deloitte Touche Tohmatsu, 2016), www2.deloitte.com/content/dam/Deloitte/global/Documents/About-Deloitte/gx-millenial-survey-2016-exec-summary.pdf.
12. Helen Bevan and Steve Fairman, "The New Era of Thinking and Practice in Change and Transformation: A Call to Action for Leaders of Health and Care," The Edge, NHS, 2014, http://theedge.nhsiq.nhs.uk/white-paper-the-new-era-of-thinking

-and-practice-in-change-and-transformation-a-call-to-action-for-leaders-of-health-and-care/.

13. "Four in 10 NHS Staff 'Made Unwell' by Work," National Health Executive, February 25, 2015, www.nationalhealthexecutive.com/Health-Care-News/four-in-10-nhs-staff-made-unwell-by-work-.
14. "When Cleveland Clinic Staff Are Troubled, They File 'Code Lavender,'" Advisory Board Daily Briefing, December 3, 2013, www.advisory.com/daily-briefing/2013/12/03/when-cleveland-clinic-staff-are-troubled-they-file-code-lavender.
15. Warren Berger, "The Power of 'Why?' and 'What If?'" *New York Times,* July 2, 2016.
16. Tim Vogus, interview with authors, December 19, 2016.
17. Frederick Hutson, interview with authors, June 11, 2015. Additional interviews were conducted in 2016 and 2017.
18. David Croft, interview with authors, October 25, 2016.
19. John Gerzema, interview with authors, June 24, 2016.
20. Deloitte, *Deloitte 2016 Millennial Survey.*
21. Josh Bersin, "Becoming Irresistible: A New Model for Employee Engagement," *Deloitte Review,* no. 16, January 26, 2015, https://dupress.deloitte.com/dup-us-en/deloitte-review/issue-16/employee-engagement-strategies.html.
22. Ivan Brincat, "Massimo Bottura Gives Lesson in Creativity: The Future Is About Culture," *Food and Wine Gazette,* October 26, 2015, www.foodandwinegazette.com/?p=4236.
23. Larry Olmsted, "The Biggest Italian Dinner in History, Thanks to Social Media," *Forbes,* October 17, 2012, www.forbes.com/sites/larryolmsted/2012/10/17/the-biggest-italian-dinner-in-history-thanks-to-social-media/#5d4469ad122b.

Chapter 8: A Bridge Over Troubled Water: The Type R Family

1. Mary Bowerman, "'France Is Our Home': Dad Tells Son Not to Be Afraid After Paris Attacks," *USA Today,* November 18, 2015.
2. Marianne Cooper, *Cut Adrift: Families in Insecure Times* (Berkeley: University of California Press, 2014).
3. Nick Stinnett and John DeFrain, *Secrets of Strong Families* (Boston: Little, Brown, 1986).
4. Suzanna Dennis and Maurice Nsabimana, interview with authors, July 2, 2015. Additional interviews were conducted in 2016.

5. W. R. Beavers and R. B. Hampson, *Successful Families: Assessment and Intervention* (New York: W. W. Norton, 1990).
6. N. Epstein, C. Ryan, D. Bishop, I. Miller, and G. Keitner, "The McMaster Model: A View of Healthy Family Functioning," in *Normal Family Processes,* 3rd ed., edited by F. Walsh, 581–607 (New York: Guilford Press, 2003).
7. J. M. Patterson and A. W. Garwick, "Levels of Meaning in Family Stress Theory," *Family Process* 33, no. 3 (1994): 287–304.
8. Kate Dyson, interview with authors, December 1, 2016.
9. Peter Yeung, "EU Referendum: Reports of Hate Crime Increase 57% Following Brexit Vote," *Independent,* June 27, 2016, www.independent.co.uk/news/uk/home-news/brexit-hate-crime-racism-reports-eu-referendum-latest-a7106116.html.
10. Sherry Turkle, *Reclaiming Conversation: The Power of Talk in a Digital Age* (New York: Penguin Press, 2015).
11. Emily Twinch, "'My French Husband Has No Respect for My Parents Any More': The Families Torn Apart by Brexit," *Independent,* June 28, 2016, www.independent.co.uk/voices/brexit-families-torn-apart-eu-referendum-my-husband-has-no-respect-for-my-family-48-per-cent-a7107096.html.

Index

Action Aid International, 128
actions
  interactions and, 114–116
  during stress, 90
  for Type R families, 211–213
  for Type R individuals, 200–204
  for Type R leaders, 205–208
  for Type R organizations, 208–211
adages, collective attitudes, 61
adaptability, 72–75, 118, 163–166
adversity
  failure, 43–46
  growth under pressure, 32–34
  meaning from, 187–188
  people affected by, 7
  positive emotions, 46–49
  reframing, 40–41, 60, 92, 124, 131–133
  responses to, 34–37
  Stephanie Decker, 29–32
  stories we tell ourselves, 37–40
  stress, advantages of, 41–43
affirming communication, 189
Afghanistan war, 102, 184
AIDS/HIV, 51–54, 58, 65
Alcoa, 141–143
Ama Marston's story, 4–6
American Psychological Association, 7
Anderson, Wendy R., 77–78, 99–102, 106, 108
appraising, 93, 94
Asch, Solomon, 140
Ashridge MBA program, United Kingdom, 146
Association of Women in Development (AWID), 129–130
assumptions, 34–35
attitudes, group, 61–62
authentic communication, 189–194

Autonomous Region of
Bougainville, 12
avoidance, 87, 94

balance, 148–149, 159–160
Barsade, Sigal, 156
Bauer, Jack, 47–48
Baum, L. Frank, 26
Beatles (music group), 20, 87
Beethoven, Ludwig van, 19
Being Wrong (Schulz), 43
beliefs, core, 141, 203
Bell, Joshua, 37
Bertolini, Mark, 140
bias-awareness training, 162
Blake, Jonathan, 51–54, 55, 61
bombings
Gaza, 17
London public transportation system, 39–40
Bonanno, George, 47–48
Bottura, Massimo, 151–154, 174–175
Bougainville, 12
Bougainville Cocoa Net Limited, 13
bouncing back, 7, 18–21
Bournville, Birmingham, England, 172
brain, studies of. *See* neuroscience
British National Health Service (NHS), 165–166
Brown, David, 59
Brown, Jerry, 22
Buddha, 103
Bush, George W., 60
business as usual
approach or solutions, 23–24
in changing times, 21–22, 127
success, view of, 24–25
uncertainty, avoiding, 22–23
business core values, 122–124, 140–141, 173

Calhoun, Lawrence, 33
California, drought (2011–2017), 21–22
Campbell, Joseph, 105
capabilities, 128–131
Carnegie Mellon University, 88
Carter, Rosalynn, 121
Carteret Atoll, 11–12
catalyst stage, of TR Journey of Change, 107
catastrophizing tendency, 93–95
Center for Creative Leadership, 128
change
business as usual and, 21–22, 127
climate change, 15, 17
embracing, 20
Type R and, 214
way forward after, 25–27
change agents, 143
chaos stage, of TR Journey of Change, 105–107
China, earthquakes in, 40
Christakis, Nicholas, 112–113
Cialdini, Robert, 114
Cleveland Clinic, 166
climate change, 15, 17
Clyde River, Canada, 139
Code Lavender (holistic health response), 166
Cohen, Sheldon, 88
collaboration, 157–158
collective consciousness, 61
collective memory bank, 209–210

collective mindset, 59–64, 156, 208–209
Collins, Jim, 167
comfort zone stage, of TR Journey of Change, 103–107
communications, 61, 143–144, 167, 189–194, 209
companies, adaptability, 74
confidence, 36, 78, 154, 183
contagion effect, 110–116
context, connecting to, 201–202
control, 75–79, 118, 144–147, 202
core beliefs and values, 141, 183, 203, 210–211
Cornell University, 137
cortisol, stress hormone, 42
counterclockwise mindset study (Harvard University), 55–57, 64
creativity, 102, 127
crisis
 as catalyst for growth, 129
 changes/responses to, 210–211
 family's experience, 180, 185–186
 glass cliff and, 85
Croft, David, 172–173
crowd mentality, 140
culture, organization's, 155–163, 209
curiosity, 80–81
curriculum vitae (CV) of failures, 204

da Vinci, Leonardo, 25
Dalai Lama, 92
Dallas, Texas
 collective mindset, 59–60
 community healing, 65, 92
 Kennedy assassination (1963), 59, 91–92
 police officers killed (2016), 59–60
 response to crisis, 91–92
D'Antonio, Michael, 126
Darwin, Charles, 20, 25, 43, 72
Decker, Stephanie, 29–31, 41
DeFrain, John, 180
Deloitte, 155, 162, 165, 174
Dennis, Suzanna, 181–182, 185–187, 195
DHEA, neurosteroid, 79
dinners, together as family, 178, 187, 192
Disney, Walt, 43–44
Disney Company, 71–72, 74
disruption stage, of TR Journey of Change, 104–105
diversity, 162–163, 165, 178
Dr. Seuss, 20
drought, in California (2011–2017), 21–22
Ducasse, Alain, 152
Duckworth, Angela, 25
Dunham, Lena, 71
Durkheim, Émile, 61
Dweck, Carol, 62–64
Dyson family (Kate, Matt, Beth, and Maggie), 190–192, 195

earthquakes
 China, Sichuan Province, 40
 Italy, Parmessian region, 175
economic inequality, 16
Edison, Charles, 44
Edison, Thomas, 20, 44
Einstein, Albert, 19, 25, 29
Eliot, George, 97
emotional contagion, 111–114
emotional hygiene, 92–93, 201

emotion-deference system, 62
emotions, 156, 193, 212
empathy, perspective and, 137, 205
employee empowerment, 207–208
engagement, 89–93, 119
European Union (EU), UK referendum on, 191
external locus of control, 75
EY (formerly Ernst and Young), 157–163

failure, 43–46, 204
family. *See* Type R family
fear, 78
fear-based reaction, 90–91
financial crisis, as limiting potential, 16
fight-or-flight response, 90–91
Ford, Henry, 23
Fowler, James, 113
Frankl, Viktor, 83–84
Fredrickson, Barbara, 48–49

Galinsky, Adam, 136–137
Gandhi, Mahatma, 89, 149
Gardner, Howard, 24
gender discrimination, 42
George Mason University, 73
Gerzema, John, 126, 173–174
Gilmore, Lara, 152–153
"glass cliff," leadership opportunity, 85
globalization, 14–15
Golden, Arthur, 67
gratefulness, 93
Greenpeace Canada, 132–133, 138–139
grit, as human characteristic, 25, 73
group attitudes, 61–62, 140, 160–161
group dynamics, 156
group support, 64, 112–113
groupthink, 165
growth
  mindset, 129
  possibility of, 94
  under pressure, 32–34
Gruber, Matthias, 80–81
Guardian (newspaper), 17

Hadid, Zaha, 44
Haley, Alex, 177
Hansen, James, 17
happiness research, 113
hardening off, plant process, 35
hardiness, as human characteristic, 25
Harry Potter (fictional character), 103
Harvard University, 24, 41–42, 55, 125
Hay, Alan, 199
health concerns
  holistic care, 166
  obesity, 135
  stress, 41–42
  technology and, 192–193
Hippocrates, 111
Hitchcock, Alfred, 48
HIV/AIDS, 51–54, 58, 65
holistic health rapid response, 166
honest communication, 189–190
hope, 65–66, 95, 196–197
hopefulness, 181–184, 213
humor, 210
Hutson, Frederick, 144–147, 169–171

identity, loss of, 101
ideology, 138
inaction, 94
individuals. *See* Type R individual
influencing and persuasion, 110–117
information flow, 167, 209
innovation, 127, 129
inquisitive thinking, 203
integration stage, of TR Journey of Change, 107–109
interconnections, 171–175
internal compass, 127, 140–144
internal locus of control, 75–76, 77, 146
Inuit community, 134, 138–139
Iraq War, 70, 102, 163–164
isolation, 87

Janis, Irving, 165
Japan, uncertainty in, 22–23
Jesus, 103
Jewish tradition, Eastern European, 80
jobs
    competition for, 15
    and economic inequality, 15–16
    job loss and effects of, 16
Jobs, Steve, 45
Journal of Positive Psychology, 81

Kahlo, Frida, 20
Kahneman, Daniel, 132
Kashdan, Todd, 73
Keller, Helen, 151
Kennedy, John F., 7, 59, 91–92
Kentucky, prosthetic parity legislation, 29–31
Kerr, Joanna, 128–130, 132–133, 137–138
Kingsolver, Barbara, 11
Kotter, John, 143

Langer, Ellen, 55–57, 64
Lawrence, Jennifer, 71
Le family (Angel and Brandon), 177
leaders and leadership
    empathy, 137
    expert leadership, 128
    facilitative, 128
    feminine style, 126
    masculine style, 126
    socially oriented, 140
    traditional, 78
    See also Type R leaders
Lear, Jonathan, 183–184
learning
    continual, 79–81, 118, 128–131
    facilitating, 210
    focus on, 203–204
    forward thinking and, 167–171
    time and resources for, 208
LGBT community
    alliance with National Union of Mineworkers (UK), 53
    EY support for, 162–163
    Jonathan Blake, 51–54
    at PepsiCo, 123–124
listening (active listening), 192–193, 212
London
    LGBT community, 51–54
    miners' strike, 52–53
    public transportation bombings, 39–40
longevity, 47, 82
Luke Skywalker (fictional character), 103

Maddi, Salvatore, 25
Major League Baseball, 114
Marshall, Barry, 23–24
Mason family (Steve, Caroline, and Amanda), 189–190
Massachusetts Institute of Technology (MIT), 193
McChrystal, Stanley, 163, 164
McKinsey & Company, 163–164
meaning, from adversity, 187–188
memory bank, collective, 209–210
mice and rats, scientific and behavioral experiments
    action during stress, 90
    rote memorization, 73
Michigan State University, 45
military service
    Afghanistan war, 102, 184
    Iraq War, 70, 102, 163–164
    PTG and, 33
Millennial generation, 7, 16, 87, 159, 165, 174
mindfulness practices, 139–140, 166
mindset
    challenges, 51–55
    collective mindset, 59–64, 208–209
    communications, 61
    as critical factor for thriving, 54
    default, 200–201
    hope and, 65–66
    for our time, 57–58
    as paradox, 55
    reality and, 55–57
miners' strike, London (1984), 52–53
mistakes, 108, 151–152
modeling positive behavior, 205
Mondelez, 172
Monet, Claude, 19
Morris Cox, Catharine, 24–25
Moser, Jason, 45–46
Moses, 103
Motherload (blog), 190
motor mimicry, 112
moving on/forward, 109–110
Murakami, Haruki, 32

National Union of Mineworkers, 53
Native American wolf story, 46
natural disasters
    drought, 21–22
    earthquakes, 40, 175
    hurricanes, 135
    tornados, 29–30
natural environment stressors, 40–41
neuroscience
    isolation and, 88
    social behavior and, 113
    stress and, 79–80
neurosteroid, DHEA, 79
new beginnings, 11–14
new capacities, 128–131
New York University, 35, 86
Newton, Sir Isaac, 20
nonfinancial incentives, 164
nonverbal messages, 190
Nooyi, Indra, 121–124, 143
Northwestern University, 136
Notre Dame School Sisters, 47
Nsabimana, Maurice, 181–182, 185–187, 195

Obama, Barack, 59–60
"Ode to Joy" (poem/symphony), 19

O'Neill, Paul, 141–143, 144
optimism, 31
organizations, 74. *See also* Type R organization
Osteria Francescana (restaurant), 151–154, 174–175
oxytocin, trust hormone, 42

pain experiment, and resilience, 76–77
Panter-Brick, Catherine, 184
parents, 211–213. *See also* Type R family
Parmesan cheese production (Italy, 2011), 175
Pennebaker, James W., 39
PepsiCo, 121–124, 143
perception, 57, 132
  stress and, 41–42
  See also perspective; vision
personal traits, 97
perspective
  adjusting, 131–140
  empathy and, 137, 205
  multifaceted, 136–140
  toughening study, 35–36
persuasion, 111–112, 114
Pigeonly company, 145–147, 168–171
Plato, 81
positive change, 33
positive emotions, 46–49
positivity, 46
post-traumatic growth (PTG), 33–34
Potter, Harry (fictional character), 103
Pritzker, Penny, 100
problems, approach or solution to, 23–24
problem-solution dichotomy, 93–95
prosthetic parity legislation, Kentucky, 29–31
psychological flexibility, 73–74
Psychological Science (journal), 45
psychological stress response, 89
PTG (post-traumatic growth), 33–34
purpose, 81–85, 118–119, 141
purpose-driven businesses, 81–85, 171–175

Quatrano, Steve, 168
questioning, 183, 200–201, 205

race relations/discrimination, 59–60, 180
radical hope, 183–184
Rakova, Ursula, 11–14
rats and mice, scientific and behavioral experiments
  action during stress, 90
  rote memorization, 73
reality, mindset and, 55–57
re-appraising, 93, 94
recalibrating, leadership compass, 124–126
Reed, Carol, 60
relational endurance, 184–187
renewal stage, of TR Journey of Change, 109
rewards, 206
Right Question Institute, 168
risk avoidance, 23
rote memorization, mice experiment, 73
Rottenberg, Jonathan, 73
Rotter, Julian, 75
Rowling, J. K., 20, 45

Ruane, Chris, (Member of Parliament, UK), 139–140
Rumi (poet), 110
rumination, 93

Satir, Virginia, 184
Scheff, Thomas, 62
Scheler, Max, 111
Schiller, Friedrich, 19
Schillinger, Celine, 165
Schulz, Kathryn, 43
Schweitzer, Albert, 127
second-order change, 106
Seery, Mark, 35–36, 76–77
self-assessment, 81
self-awareness, 81, 137
self-care, 212
self-narratives, 37–40, 104
self-reflection, 101–102
Serrato, Yolanda, 21
Settecase, Michelle, 157–160
Shakespeare, William, 51, 81
Simonton, Dean Keith, 92
Skywalker, Luke (fictional character), 103
Smith, Adam, 112
Snyder, C. R., 66
social network, 112–113
social validation/proof, 114
socially responsible businesses, 81–85, 171–175
soft skills, 158
Solis, Miguel, 60
Solnit, Rebecca, 65
Sotomayor, Sonia, 97–98
Southwick, Steven M., 38
Spielberg, Steven, 20
springing forward, 18–21, 47
Stanford University, 45, 79
status quo, 21–22, 125, 165
Stefan, Melanie, 204
Stephanie Marston's story, 2–4
Stiglitz, Joseph, 14–15
Stinnett, Nick, 180
stories
    family culture through, 211
    self-narratives, 37–40, 104
stress
    control and, 76
    neurosteroid and, 79
    people affected by, 7
    perception and, 41–42
    toughening study, 35–36
success, view of, 24–25
superheroes, 33
support network, 85–89, 119, 194–195, 211, 213
sustainability, 20–21, 114–115, 122–124
SWOT analyses, 207

Taka (Osteria Francescana sous-chef), 151–152
talent, success and, 24–25
technology, communication and, 192–193
Tedeschi, Richard, 33
terrorism, acts of
    Gaza school bombing, 17
    London public transportation bombings (2005), 39–40
    Nigeria kidnappings, 17
    Paris attack (2015), 177
    September 11, 2001, 58, 99
Thatcher, Margaret, 52
Thompson, Akira, 70–73, 74
time, for learning, 208
Tippett, Krista, 17
Toffler, Alvin, 79
Tolstoy, Leo, 17
tornados, 29–30
toughening study, 35–36, 76

traits, personal, 97
Transformative Resilience (TR), 2, 8–9, 18–20
  and failure, 43
  obstacles to, 21–25
  and positivity, 46–47
  and stress, 33, 36
  See also TR Journey of Change; *individual entries for Type R*
TR Journey of Change
  catalyst stage, 107
  chaos stage, 105–107
  comfort zone stage, 103–104
  disruption stage, 104–105
  integration stage, 107–109
  renewal stage, 109
trust hormone, oxytocin, 42
Turkle, Sherry, 193
turnover, leadership, 126
20-Mile March, 146
Type R in action
  for families, 211–213
  for individuals, 200–204
  for leaders, 205–208
  for organizations, 208–211
  overview, 199–200
Type R characteristics
  adaptability, 72–75
  control, 75–79
  engagement, 89–93
  learning, 79–81
  Mary Poppins analogy, 67–68
  overview, 69–72
  purpose, 81–85
  support network, 85–89
Type R family
  actions for, 211–213
  challenges, 178
  characteristics, 179–181
  communication, 189–194
  future hope, 196–197
  hopefulness, 181–184
  Le family, 177
  meaning, from adversity, 187–188
  relational endurance, 184–187
  support structures, 194–195
Type R individual
  actions for, 200–204
  contagion effect, 110–116
  journey, 99–103, 109–110
  power of, 116–117
  self-assessment of, 117–120
  stages, 103–110
Type R leaders
  actions for, 205–208
  balance, 148–149
  capabilities, 128–131
  changing times, 126–127
  internal compass, 140–144
  leadership compass, recalibrating, 124–126
  learning continuously, 128–131
  perspective, adjusting, 131–140
  sense of control, 144–147
Type R organization
  actions for, 208–211
  adaptability, 163–166
  culture, 155–163, 209
  interconnections, 171–175
  learning, 167–174
  overview, 154–155
Type R quotient, 117–120
Type R vision
  agile framing and reframing, 131–133
  kaleidoscope (multifaceted perspective), 136–140
  near and far, 133–134

Type R vision *(continued)*
    perspective, 136–140
    present and future, 133–134
    speed and timing, 134–136

ulcers, cause of, 23–24
uncertainty
    avoiding, 22–23
    embracing, 127
    era of, 14–18
    hope and, 65–66
United Kingdom
    Ashridge MBA program, 146
    Bournville community, 172
    EU referendum, 191
    London bombings, 39–40
    London miners' strike, 52–53
University of California, 62, 72, 80, 92
University of Cape Town, 146
University of Edinburgh, 204
University of Groningen, Netherlands, 73
University of Louisville, 30
University of North Carolina, 33, 48
University of Oxford, 129
University of Pennsylvania, 30
University of South Florida, 73
University of Texas, 39
University of Virginia, 171–172
University of Washington, 171–172

values (clarifying principles or standards of behavior), 183, 203, 210–211
Van Gogh, Vincent, 20
Vanderbilt University, 164
viewpoints, 37, 211–212
violent conflicts
    Dallas police officers, 59–60
    Gaza bombings, 17
    Iraq War, 70, 102, 163–164
    Nigeria kidnappings, 17
vision, 116, 207
    agile framing and reframing, 131–133
    kaleidoscope (multifaceted perspective), 136–140
    near and far, present and future, 133–134
    speed and timing, 134–136, 169
    See also perception; perspective; Type R vision
Vogus, Tim, 164, 168

Warby Parker glasses, 83
Warhol, Andy, 171
Warren, Jill, 85–87, 93
wealth, 16
Weinberger, Mark, 157–158
Weingarten, Gene, 37
Whyte, David, 141
Wizard of Oz, 26
wolf story, 46
women's math skills, 62–64
Wozniak, Steve, 19

Yale University, 38, 156, 184
Yousafzai, Malala, 115–116

Zolli, Andrew, 20

About the Authors

Ama Marston © JD Marston

Ama Marston is an international strategy and leadership expert as well as a recognized thought leader focused on Transformative Resilience and inclusive and purpose-driven leadership and business. She is the founder of Marston Consulting, which has provided services to FTSE and Fortune 500 companies, the United Nations, University of Oxford, and numerous others. Her previous work with leaders such as Mary Robinson, Ireland's first female president, and Joseph Stiglitz, the Nobel laureate economist, and as a top adviser to international NGOs has placed her at numerous decision-making tables and taken her to work in countries around the world. She earned a master's degree from Columbia University and has long been hailed as a leader and original thinker. She has won several awards, including Phi Beta Kappa national honors and a Council of Women World Leaders Fellowship. She is the daughter of coauthor Stephanie Marston and splits her time between London and the United States.

Stephanie Marston © Eric Swanson

Stephanie Marston is a nationally recognized resilience and work/life expert. She has appeared frequently on shows such as *The Oprah Show, The Today Show, CNN Headline News,* and numerous other radio and TV programs. She is a five-time published author and a psychotherapist with more than thirty years of experience. She is the founder of 30 Days to Sanity, a stress and work/life online platform. She has served on the WebMD clinical advisory board. Some of her clients include Whirlpool Corporation, McDonald's Corporation, H. J. Heinz Company, Xerox Corporation, Mattel, Prudential Insurance, Morgan Stanley, and The Mayo Clinic. Stephanie lives in Santa Fe, New Mexico, and is the mother of coauthor Ama Marston.

PublicAffairs is a publishing house founded in 1997. It is a tribute to the standards, values, and flair of three persons who have served as mentors to countless reporters, writers, editors, and book people of all kinds, including me.

I. F. STONE, proprietor of *I. F. Stone's Weekly*, combined a commitment to the First Amendment with entrepreneurial zeal and reporting skill and became one of the great independent journalists in American history. At the age of eighty, Izzy published *The Trial of Socrates*, which was a national bestseller. He wrote the book after he taught himself ancient Greek.

BENJAMIN C. BRADLEE was for nearly thirty years the charismatic editorial leader of *The Washington Post*. It was Ben who gave the *Post* the range and courage to pursue such historic issues as Watergate. He supported his reporters with a tenacity that made them fearless and it is no accident that so many became authors of influential, best-selling books.

ROBERT L. BERNSTEIN, the chief executive of Random House for more than a quarter century, guided one of the nation's premier publishing houses. Bob was personally responsible for many books of political dissent and argument that challenged tyranny around the globe. He is also the founder and longtime chair of Human Rights Watch, one of the most respected human rights organizations in the world.

• • •

For fifty years, the banner of Public Affairs Press was carried by its owner Morris B. Schnapper, who published Gandhi, Nasser, Toynbee, Truman, and about 1,500 other authors. In 1983, Schnapper was described by *The Washington Post* as "a redoubtable gadfly." His legacy will endure in the books to come.

Peter Osnos, *Founder*